MORAL THEORY AND CAPITAL PUNISHMENT

TOM SORELL

Basil Blackwell
in association with the
Open University

First published 1987
First published in USA 1988

Basil Blackwell Ltd
108 Cowley Road, Oxford, OX4 1JF, UK

Basil Blackwell Inc.
432 Park Avenue South, Suite 1503
New York, NY 10016, USA

British Library Cataloguing in Publication Data
Sorell, Tom
Moral theory and capital punishment.
1. Capital punishment—Moral and
ethical aspects
I. Title
179'.7 HV8694

ISBN 0-631-15321-7
ISBN 0-631-15322-5 Pbk

Library of Congress Cataloging in Publication Data
Sorell, Tom.
Moral theory and capital punishment.

Includes index.
1. Capital punishment—Moral and ethical aspects.
I. Title.
HV8694.S67 1987 179'.7 87-20866
ISBN 0-631-15321-7
ISBN 0-631-15322-5 (pbk.)

This book forms part of an Open University course, *A310 Life and Death*.
For further information about this course, please write to the
Student Enquiries Office, The Open University, PO Box 71,
Walton Hall, Milton Keynes, MK7 6AG, UK

Typeset in 11 on 12½ point Bembo
by Photo·Graphics, Honiton, Devon
Printed in Great Britain by Page Bros Ltd, Norwich

Contents

Preface

This is a book about the morality of capital punishment and the application of philosophical theories of right and wrong. In the first two chapters I argue that philosophical theories of right and wrong can be useful in producing an improved moral rhetoric, that is, a kind of persuasion that is more rigorous and even-handed than the sort to be found in lobbyists' pamphlets or ordinary conversation. Philosophically informed rhetoric can, of course, have conclusions in common with the more familiar forms of rhetoric – it can oppose the practice of abortion, for example, or support the practice of euthanasia – but its premises are likely to be more general and more systematically worked out. When all goes well it is persuasive without being shallow and consistent without being boring.

In saying that philosophical theories of right and wrong can be used to improve moral rhetoric, I mean to disagree with those who say that philosophy should only lend techniques of reasoning to moral debate, and not take sides. It is true that philosophy can improve debate by making people aware of its standards of constructing and criticizing arguments. It is not necessarily true that when applied these standards will show that opposing positions in a debate are equally strong. It is perfectly possible that some arguments will be better than others. There is no reason why philosophers should not say so and take sides accordingly. Even where the arguments are evenly balanced the right stance to adopt need not be one of neutrality. It can once again be legitimate to take sides, so long as one is prepared to acknowledge the strengths of the opposing view. Tolerance rather than neutrality seems to be the right value to promote in applying moral theory to rhetoric.

Capital punishment receives two kinds of treatment in this book. First it is discussed as one among other kinds of killing that philosophers, lobbyists and others sometimes try to justify. Then arguments special to the death penalty are reviewed. Utilitarian arguments for and against are considered, and there is a detailed examination of the claim that execution is wrong because it is a cruel and unusual punishment. Eventually I come out in favour of the death penalty, but only for a narrow class of murders. The framework I adopt for stating and defending my position is Kant's, though mine is a less sweeping endorsement of capital punishment for murder than Kant's own. At the end I acknowledge difficulties for framing appropriate legislation, notwithstanding the fact that a strong moral argument for capital punishment can be given.

Acknowledgements

This book is part of an Open University course in applied ethics. Colleagues on the course team have made useful suggestions and criticisms. In particular, I should like to thank Godfrey Vesey and Peter Wright. I am also grateful to two philosophers at other universities. John Harris produced valuable comments on the penultimate draft, and Michael Lockwood is responsible for a host of improvements throughout. Quartet Books kindly gave permission for use of the quotation from Doug Magee, *Slow Coming Dark* (Quartet Books, 1987).

CHAPTER ONE

Killing: moral rhetoric and moral philosophy

1 PERMISSIBLE KILLING

If the loss of human life is always unfortunate, must it not be more than unfortunate – evil – for human life to be taken deliberately? It is often thought to be evil. Yet is it so evil that it must be avoided at all costs? If so, then suicide must be avoided at all costs. Euthanasia and capital punishment must be avoided at all costs. Abortion, war, and the assassination of a Hitler or an Amin must be avoided at all costs. The sweeping consequences of an absolute prohibition may make us think twice. *Is* it true that one must avoid taking human life no matter what? Or may there, in certain circumstances, be good reasons for killing that make it morally permissible in spite of what is otherwise wrong with taking human life?

These questions have more than theoretical interest, because many people have experience of situations in which taking life seems a real, even a reasonable, option. Unwanted pregnancies are not uncommon, and the fact that a pregnancy is unwanted gives a reason, though perhaps not a decisive reason, for having an abortion. Wars and military adventures are not uncommon. When they are in a cause people can agree to be good, the cause seems to justify the taking of life. People who lack direct experience of unwanted pregnancy or military service in wartime can often imagine themselves in such situations, and can confront vicariously the questions they raise. And they can put themselves in other circumstances calling for life and death decisions as well. For example, many generally stable people suffer depressions that make suicide thinkable, however occasionally or fleetingly.

Again, many people have jobs that can lead them to consider either taking life or doing nothing to prevent it ending. Nurses, police officers, doctors, lawyers and judges may be attracted in theory to the idea that killing is never right and yet they may be faced with situations that seem to demand or permit the taking of human life, situations that require them to act. Since it is important for people to be able to justify to themselves and to other people what they are prepared to do, and since standards of justification are likely to be particularly exacting when lives are in the balance, it should matter particularly to people in law or medicine or allied fields whether taking life is always or only sometimes wrong. It should also matter to the rest of us, who have to be able to justify to ourselves and to other people what we are prepared to stand back and *see* done. Everyone, it seems, has a stake in the question of whether killing people is always wrong.

So much for the question. The answer appears to be that it is *not* always wrong, that the prohibition on killing people has exceptions. Take, for example, killing in self-defence, or killing in a case where not to do so would mean a lingering, painful death for someone whose life cannot be saved anyway. These cases seem to tell against an absolute prohibition. They seem to show that taking human life is not always but perhaps only usually wrong. But if killing people is permissible in some cases and not in others, which cases are which? Is it possible to qualify the principle that killing people is always wrong and still be left with a principle that tells us *when* it is wrong?

If we are looking for a single qualified principle to take the place of the absolute prohibition on killing, one that is not merely the conjunction of a lot of different principles, then we are likely to be in for a disappointment. This is because different exceptions to the absolute prohibition recommend themselves for different reasons, which a revised principle cannot unify all at once. For example, killing a dying person who is in unrelievable agony may be permissible, because the quality of the rest of his life may be so bad as to make him better off dead. Killing in self-defence may be all right, because in doing so one is reacting against the evil of a life-threatening attack, not just saving one's own skin at the expense of someone else's. These grounds for allowable killing are not easy to put together. Consequently, it may be unreasonable to hope for a principle that says simply and directly when killing is permitted and when it is not. It may be that general moral guidance about allowable killing must take the form of a plurality of principles.[1]

2 PRINCIPLES AND THEIR SOURCES

What counts as a principle in the present context, and where are principles bearing on life and death decisions to be found? By a 'principle' I mean a reason for doing or omitting something, a reason that is, in the first place, general. It must apply in a wide range of situations. It must also be acceptable to many people. 'Because it would mean lying' expresses a possible reason in this sense for my omitting to do something, say, writing down an exaggerated expense claim on my tax return. It brings to bear on a particular situation the generally applicable consideration that it is wrong to lie. Other reasons for action are too specific to be generally applicable or generally acceptable and so have a weaker claim to express principles. The fact that Jenny wants one may be a reason for Jenny's best friend to buy her a micro-computer, but it will not constitute a reason for many other people to buy Jenny a micro-computer, or indeed to do much else. Further facts about Jenny, as yet unspecified, could, perhaps, make it appropriate for others to buy her a micro-computer. For example, it could be a fact that Jenny has talents as an engineer or scientist and that she needs a personal computer to help her to exercise her talents. This fact is a reason to get Jenny a micro-computer if it is in general right to help people to exercise their talents. But the general reason, even if it is found compelling, is not about Jenny in particular. It is about helping talented people whoever they are. This sort of generality is characteristic of principles.[2]

Principles that give guidance in decisions about life and death are often moral principles. When does a general reason for action qualify as a moral principle? A stock answer is, when the general reason could be *any* sane adult's reason for an action or omission, and when, by acting on the reason, one would be promoting the well-being of others. This is not an impeccable formulation,[3] but let us accept it for now and ask where we turn for moral principles that can guide us in life and death decisions.

Moral education and experience

One source of moral principles is each person's upbringing and education, modified by that person's experience of life. It is unclear, however, whether this important source of moral principles provides adequate guidance for life and death decisions. Many people with a standard upbringing and education, and with an ordinary store of experience, are brought up short by cases in which killing or allowing someone to die does not appear to be cruel or in which the reasons for having an abortion are not merely selfish. Faced with such cases people can feel torn between the belief that killing is wrong, and the thought that the reasons in favour of taking or ending a life are quite compelling. Of course, the feeling of being torn is not confined to life and death decisions. Cases quite outside that area can also seem difficult to form judgements about on the basis of one's moral education. For example, most people believe that it is wrong to lie and also that it is wrong to offend people. But in certain situations, apparently, it is not possible both to be sincere and to spare people's feelings. I hope it will be agreed that while such situations arise, and while they are difficult to handle properly, they do not strain ordinary moral education and experience in anything like the way life and death decisions do. Though they present real dilemmas, the things in the balance, namely the wrongness of lying and the badness of being offended, count for far less than considerations about outright loss of life or severely reduced quality of life. It is because it is hard for us to see what could matter *more* than these things that decisions or judgements involving them seem especially difficult to make.

Before considering the idea that we have to look outside ordinary moral education and experience for help with decisions and judgements about life and death, it is worth taking up two views which suggest that no such casting about is necessary. One of the views I have in mind is that decisions and judgements about life and death are not for us to make anyway, that we are really usurping God's office when we deliberate about, let alone go through with, an abortion or a so-called mercy killing. It may be in order for us to pray that God be merciful in decreeing the relevant outcome, but it is really in His hands, and we should rather let nature take its course than give weight in our deliberations to the option of taking life ourselves. One way in which this line of thought invites dispute is by assuming the existence of a God whose office is usurped when human beings deliberate about taking life. But even if it is agreed that God exists, the view seems open to question in the light of cases that tell against an absolute prohibition on killing. If we must never consider taking human life we must never do so when our own lives are at stake, or when someone whose death is unpreventable, and who is suffering horribly, begs to be finished off.

The second view I want to consider does not put life and death decisions out of bounds to human beings. It supposes that ordinary moral education equips people to decide questions of life and death satisfactorily, and it traces indecision in the face of hard cases to influences that distract us from, or entice us to ignore, the demands of morality as taught. The idea is that our moral education pronounces clearly until our judgement is clouded by extraneous influences, such as selfish personal desires, or a corrupting social climate – the 'permissive society' as it is sometimes called. Thus it might be said that a prohibition on taking human life is part of our standard moral education, and that the prohibition extends straightforwardly to taking the life of a fœtus or killing the terminally ill at their request. If in particular cases it seems there might be reasons in favour of abortion or euthanasia, then that is an illusion produced by some unsavoury social attitudes, such as a growing unwillingness to look after the very young or the terminally ill, or the selfish desires of individuals who, for example, put their careers ahead of everything and everybody else.

There is no doubt something in the suggestion that indecision results from a conflict between selfish desires and morality, or a conflict between unsavoury attitudes and morality, rather than from a conflict between the demands of morality themselves. But it begs the question to say that it is always selfishness or a corrupting social climate that throws the dust in our eyes. Again, and contrary to what is assumed by the view we are considering, it does not follow that if one's moral education pronounces clearly on life and death issues, it pronounces correctly. On the contrary, the fact that it pronounces clearly may be due to its leaving out of the reckoning features of life and death decisions that ought to matter. Perhaps the clarity is made possible by moral complacency or simplemindedness. Even where it is not, and the directives of one's moral education really do settle questions satisfactorily, there ought usually to be some reason for this independent of the fact that the directives are clear or familiar. No one would give as a justification for holding a particular non-moral belief 'I've been taught to think so' or 'That's what it comes naturally to me to think'. There is no reason to expect such a 'defence' of a particular moral reaction to be satisfactory either.

Looking beyond moral education and experience

Several reasons have emerged for looking beyond one's moral education and experience for help with life and death decisions. First, moral education and experience do not always deliver clear answers to questions about taking human life. Where clear answers are forthcoming, they need not be correct. When the answers seem correct, it may be unclear why they do. If these are ways in which moral education and experience can fall short, what other source of moral advice is there? The prevailing legal code is sometimes a guide to practice in areas where one's moral education does not pronounce clearly – certain areas of business dealing, for example. But since people's decisions about life and death issues can call into question the morality of the relevant law itself, the prevailing legal code may not be able to give advice with enough authority. Where else are people to turn? If they are professionally involved in life and death decisions they are sometimes subject to their own professional codes of conduct and statements of the rights of patients and offenders.[4] These, too, however, can be subject to the limitations of the wider body of law, and, in any case, they are not addressed to everyone who has a stake in life and death decisions. I shall discuss two other sources of moral guidance: the rhetoric of life and death lobbies or interest groups on the one hand, and the branch of moral philosophy called 'normative ethics' on the other.

3 THE RHETORIC OF LIFE AND DEATH

By 'rhetoric' I mean public statements by which certain people try to bring others round to their point of view. The rhetoric of life and death consists of public statements issued by those who have made up their minds about the permissibility of, for example, abortion, euthanasia or capital punishment – statements intended to persuade others to think as they do. 'Public statement' needs to be interpreted broadly, so that it includes not only pamphlets, leaflets, newspaper articles, novels and so on, but also slogans chanted at demonstrations, car bumper and windscreen stickers, posters, lapel buttons, tee-shirts, films, videos, television programmes and advertisements. Standardly, the views expressed in any of these ways will be those of an interest group or lobby rather than of a particular individual, but it will do no harm to suppose that there can be a one-woman or one-man campaign of persuasion. In the same way, we need not be restrictive in our assumptions about the intended audience for a piece of rhetoric. As a rule, a persuasive public statement will be directed at as many people as are willing to listen, but it can make sense for its target to be a committee of a few people or an occupational group made up of several hundred thousand.

Persuasive public statements often take the form of arguments to certain conclusions; when they take other forms they can often be reinterpreted as pieces of reasoning. Following Aristotle, who was one of the first people to give a comprehensive theory of it, we can say that rhetoric is a kind of reasoning that starts from things an audience already believes, and proceeds to conclusions that they do not already believe, but that the giver of the reasoning wants them to believe, in the ideal case, for their own good. Moral rhetoric is argument to or from beliefs about what is right or wrong, just or unjust, good or evil. Later on I shall quote and discuss some samples of moral rhetoric from both sides of the periodically re-opened public and parliamentary debate on capital punishment in Britain. But I shall assume that readers have encountered other rhetorical statements about life and death issues, issues as different as abortion and nuclear disarmament, as well as rhetoric about a host of other matters, from the restriction of trade-union rights to cigarette-smoking and the compulsory wearing of seatbelts in motor cars.

Effective rhetoric must first capture attention and then convince. It may do both and yet present a bad argument for whatever point of view is being promoted. It may, for example, exploit false or disputable beliefs an audience already holds. It may manipulate people's emotions, turning unfocused distress or unease into fear or dislike of some identifiable group or person, without the fear or dislike having any sound basis. These latter effects are probably most readily associated with the rhetoric of racialist and sectarian groups and parties. But it is possible for false beliefs to be traded upon and for ill-grounded emotions to be stirred up in a good cause as well. In such cases a position that there may be compelling reasons for accepting may in fact be accepted on the strength of a vivid but false analogy, a striking photograph or poster, or the looks of the television presenter who is got to speak on its behalf. I may be indifferent to the latest research reports confirming the dangers of cigarettes, and yet be persuaded to give up smoking by a poster that exploits my embarrassment at the sight of nicotine stains on my fingers. The poster may do the trick and get me to break my habit even if, in fact, no one else has ever noticed the nicotine stains and I have no real ground for embarrassment.[5]

Rhetoric about the more dramatic life and death issues can also persuade for the wrong reasons. Let me illustrate with a device used by both sides in the controversy over the permissibility of abortion. It is sometimes said by those in favour of abortion that the fœtus is not a person, and that this fact makes it nonsense to say of a fœtus that it has rights in general, or a right to life in particular. In reply, members of the anti-abortion lobby sometimes produce photographs or film in which fœtuses are hard to distinguish from babies at birth. I take it that the message of the photographs, in the context of the anti-abortion argument, is roughly as follows: 'These fœtuses are as good as indistinguishable from babies, and babies undoubtedly have a right to life: why then haven't fœtuses a right to life?' Though I do not for a moment deny that photographs or film with this message can be persuasive, even decisive, in making people oppose abortion, the message of the photographs and film as I understand it, is question-begging. What the photographs show are beings visually similar to, let us even say indistinguishable from, newborn babies, who (let us say again) are indisputably creatures with a right to life. Still, and to come to the question begged, looking just like a creature who indisputably has the right to life and is a person, is neither necessary nor sufficient for having a right to life or for being a person. If it were sufficient, then a lifelike robot would qualify for civil rights. If it were necessary, then the badly deformed or badly mutilated would not count as persons. Of course, rhetoric that uses photographs of baby-like fœtuses is not unique in begging the question. Photographs of cell-clumps are equally question-begging as evidence *against* the claim that fœtuses are persons, since what may be at issue is whether the cell-clumps become persons.

Moral rhetoric and moral guidance

The fact that a piece of rhetoric about life and death can trade on false beliefs or employ questionable forms of argument does not mean that it must do so, or even that it typically does. Where the audience is reasonably well-informed or capable of checking facts, where they have a nose for exaggeration, it pays someone with a job of persuasion to do to get the facts straight and stick to them. It also pays to keep the form of argument clear and above board. We need not assume that because departures from the facts and from logic are tolerated by the aim of persuasion, that producers of rhetoric are bound to distort facts or mangle logic. Even when they do not, however, moral rhetoric can have shortcomings as a source of moral guidance.

To begin with, there can be powerful rhetoric on *both* sides of a controversy. This means that the indecision one feels when one privately considers, say, the rights and wrongs of abortion, can be reproduced when the matter is thrashed out in public by the lobbyists. Of course, the parties to the public controversy may be able to formulate the principles on each side more clearly than one is able to do oneself. But this is not necessarily a help, since the conflicting principles may not be easy to weigh on a single scale. In the controversy over the permissibility of abortion, for example, the principle of respect for persons (including the fœtus) is often opposed to the principle that one should be able to decide what happens to one's own body. People who argue from these principles do not seem to be arguing in the same terms, and it is not obvious what can be done to bridge the gap. The problem is not solved but aggravated by translating the rival principles into what looks like a common terminology of rights; for not only is it unclear how one is to juxtapose 'woman's right to choose' with 'the right to life of the unborn', it is not always clear what content talk of rights has in this and other contexts. Cannot the claim 'I have a right to it' just be a tendentious way of saying one wants it badly? Might not life be a condition of having rights, rather than something one has a right to? Both questions are ways of indicating the strains in rhetorical talk of rights.

In addition to the problem of being certain that the terms used have a clear sense and that the principles are commensurable or able to be weighed on a single scale, there is a problem of narrowness. Moral rhetoric, at least as practised by life and death lobbies or interest groups, tends to be narrowly focused. The lobby that concerns itself with abortion may be silent on capital punishment, and the lobby in favour of making it legal to assist suicides may have nothing to say about the rights and wrongs of experimenting with embryos or the morality of war. Often, however, a principle that is invoked in rhetoric about one issue will have consequences for another – consequences that affect the acceptability of the principle in general. For instance, the principle of the sanctity of life can be a reason for believing in the impermissibility of abortion. But many people who believe in the impermissibility of abortion believe at the same time in the permissibility of capital punishment for murderers. This position is inconsistent if one believes in the sanctity of human life, for if every human life is sacred so must the life of every human murderer be sacred. A more restricted principle – that all innocent human life is sacred – may prevent the tension just noted from arising, but the restricted principle may not keep fresh trouble from cropping up elsewhere. To illustrate, suppose that there is only a single dose of a certain drug, and that there is a choice between giving it to a badly wounded murderer and saving his life, and giving it to an innocent person and saving this person from some moderate pain. Would the fact that no innocent life would be lost excuse giving the dose to the person in pain rather than the dying murderer? Questions like this, which test the acceptability of principles outside the area in which they are chosen to apply, are likely to be missed when rhetoric is narrowly focused.

So it pays to widen the scope. But not all ways of widening it will be helpful. The distinctions between liberal and conservative, for example, and between socialist and capitalist, classify a wide range of views on issues of public interest, but they do not seem to give the right sort of broad perspective on the whole range of questions about killing. For one thing, they tend to add to rather than take away from the controversialness of the questions. Furthermore, these political distinctions do not always coincide with the main lines of moral disagreement. Political conservatives not only disagree with liberals, they often differ amongst themselves in their attitudes to questions about killing. On the other hand, socialists and capitalists who are otherwise at odds may well agree in their views about the morality of suicide or euthanasia. In short, positions in the debate about the rights and wrongs of killing cut across the left/right divide. Even where one pattern of views about killing is characteristic of a liberal position and another is distinctive of a conservative position, it can be a question whether the pattern of views is internally consistent. Thus, it can be a question whether the characteristic conservative is consistent to oppose abortion and support capital punishment, and it can be a question whether the standard liberal is consistent in supporting abortion and opposing capital punishment. The left/right and liberal/conservative distinctions are not cut out for highlighting relations of consistency, but clarity about these relations is necessary if the problem of narrowness is to be solved.

Finally, and related to the problem of narrowness, there is a problem of depth of justification in moral rhetoric. Suppose someone argues for hanging convicted murderers by saying that hanging will deter more potential murderers and save more potential victims' lives than other less severe forms of punishment. In the face of such an argument it will normally be in order to ask for statistical evidence showing a difference in murder rates between the places or times in which the death penalty is in force and places or times in which it is not. But consider a request for quite a different sort of justification, which most people see the point of once it has been expressed. Suppose someone asks why numbers should matter at all. Does the fact that three people will live if one is killed justify or excuse killing the one? Deference to numbers may minimize the worth of a single life. This type of objection, which invites justification for a justification of capital punishment, that is, justification for the justification that it will maximize lives saved, is usually left out of ordinary rhetoric about life and death for no better reason than that it is slightly abstract. But if moral rhetoric stays down to earth at the cost of failing to justify principles which it invokes, it may not deserve to persuade.

4 MORAL PHILOSOPHY: NORMATIVE ETHICS

Moral philosophy solves some of the problems of moral rhetoric and makes headway with others. One branch of the subject – meta-ethics – is devoted to clarifying moral concepts such as that of a right. It also makes explicit the nature of moral justification, and exhibits correct patterns of moral reasoning. This is the branch of moral philosophy that can be expected to sharpen talk of, for example 'the right to life'. But it is mainly concerned with the clarification of concepts used in talking about morality, not with arriving at substantive moral judgements. So while it may tell us what a right is, meta-ethics will not tell us whether a fœtus has rights violated through abortion. And while it may tell us what justice is, it will not tell us whether it is just to put murderers to death.

In order to settle these substantive questions one needs substantive moral principles and these come from normative ethics. This branch of moral philosophy tells us, among other things, whether it is ever right to kill, and if so, in what cases. Its principles can be expected to justify judgements about other actions in various situations, and not just judgements about killing. The morality of a host of things – from civil disobedience to the disclosure of confidential information to extra-marital sex – can be discussed by this second branch of moral philosophy.

Since a normative ethical theory states and defends principles that bear on life and death decisions, and since such a theory, when informed by a suitable meta-ethics, can be expected to minimize illogicality, narrowness and shallowness of justification, it may look like the sort of theory that ought to guide us *instead* of moral rhetoric in matters of life and death. Perhaps instead of making up our minds in the light of a public debate whose terms are set by lobbies and interest groups, we would do better to consult normative ethics. If this means submitting specific practical questions to normative ethics rather than to moral rhetoric, it may be a misguided suggestion. For one thing, there is no guarantee that the principles of a normative theory will apply to a particular, practical question. Worse, there is no guarantee against two conflicting theories applying to the same question. A normative ethical theory that does apply and give guidance, may be competing with another normative ethical theory that also applies and gives different advice. 'Normative ethics' is not the name of a single system of principles which discriminates right from wrong actions; it covers a number of such systems, not all of them compatible.

Again, when a particular normative ethical theory does provide definite guidance, its advice is not necessarily different from that of a piece of moral rhetoric. This is because moral rhetoric standardly draws on one or another normative ethical theory, or on principles organized by such a theory. Moral rhetoric may not always make the relevant theory or principles explicit, and rhetoricians may appeal to the theory or the principles without realizing it. Some acquaintance with moral philosophy may be required to identify the sort of outlook that the rhetoric articulates. But it would be a mistake to suppose that moral rhetoric operates with a set of principles necessarily distinct from, and in competition with, those of recognized theories in moral philosophy. The recognized theories are the source of much that is general in moral rhetoric, that is, the principles it invokes, and it is in the practice of rhetoric, that is, in the heat of public debate about the rightness and wrongness of certain actions, that normative ethical theories are themselves extended and revised.

What are the benefits?

If normative ethics does not necessarily give specific or uniform moral guidance, let alone moral guidance distinct from that of moral rhetoric, how, if at all, can it help? I suggested earlier that it might improve on ordinary moral rhetoric by stating very general reasons for actions or omissions, reasons which give deeper justification than the common run of statements about right and wrong. The deeper reasons may sometimes be controversial, but even where they are, they can provide clearer and more precise grounding for judgements and actions than ordinary public debate. This clarity and precision can set a beneficial example. The more widely recognized the moral principles of contending positions and the more widely recognized the consequences of those principles, including implausible principles and implausible consequences, the less likely it is that people will be swayed gratuitously when those principles are invoked by politicians and interest groups. The effects of a diminished power of persuasion can be significant in practice, for votes in elections and votes on legislation can depend on how easy it is to win people over.

Another thing that normative ethics can do is discourage the rush to judgement. Before lobbyists accuse certain nurses, doctors, judges and juries of cold-blooded murder, before they complain of the violation of women's rights or the rights of the victims of crime, they should know whether systematic justification can be given for the views or actions they disapprove of. If it can be, normative ethics will often show as much. And if there is systematic justification for the actions or views at issue, there is systematic justification for tolerating them. There is further justification for tolerance if the people whose acts are in question are reasonably conscientious and if they have to act in a hurry with scarce resources.

To those with strong views on life and death issues the creation of tolerance may be hard to distinguish from the erosion of moral standards or the encouragement of a general permissiveness. If under the guise of fostering tolerance normative ethics really promotes the view that anything goes, then far from doing any good, it may actually do more harm than the most underhand moral rhetoric. In fact, however, the creation of moral tolerance only makes sense on the assumption that *not* just anything goes. The assumptions appropriate to the sort of toleration under discussion are these: that there are right and wrong answers to moral questions, that the right answers are hard to find, that nothing qualifies as a possible right answer unless good reasons or an argument can be given for it, and that good reasons and good arguments can be given for more than one answer. In the view appropriate to blank permissiveness, on the other hand, there only *appear* to be moral questions with right and wrong answers. In fact, there only *appear* to be moral problems; for given any two conflicting courses of action one is always as good as the other. This view makes pointless the very thing that the other position counts as crucial, namely an argument or reason that establishes one course of action or solution as the right one.

Suppose creating tolerance is not thought to be tantamount to saying that anything goes; suppose it is seen as a genuine benefit. Does normative ethics really confer this benefit? There are philosophers who doubt it. Some would go further to claim that moral philosophy clouds our understanding of what we should do and how we should live. This view about the limits of moral philosophy has a loose counterpart in a view about philosophy in general – to the effect that philosophy has no practical implications it can call its own, to the effect that the idea of applied philosophy is somehow confused. For reasons that will emerge presently, I believe that both views are mistaken. However, they are closer to the truth than others which suggest that philosophers have a special vocation to resolve problems of moral value in general and concrete ethical dilemmas in particular. The good that philosophy can do seems to be modest – modest but not negligible.

5 DISTRUSTING MORAL THEORY

It is sometimes claimed that moral theory derived from philosophy is of no use, and in particular that it cannot operate as a proper source of justification. The worry is not (or not just) that moral theory tries to justify too *many* moral claims or beliefs; it is that, in trying to justify any it lays stress on general, relatively contentless reasons for action or omission, whereas what we may need is ethical material that can animate our lives and inspire commitment. Bernard Williams puts over this view where he says that critical reflection on ethical life

> should basically go in a direction opposite to that encouraged by ethical theory. Theory looks characteristically for considerations that are very general and have as little distinctive content as possible, because it is trying to systematize and because it wants to represent as many reasons as possible as applications of other reasons. But critical reflection should seek for as much shared understanding as it can find on any issue, and use any ethical material that, in the context of the reflective discussion, makes some sense and commands some loyalty. Of course, that will take some things for granted, but as serious reflection it must know it will do that. The only serious enterprise is living, and we have to live after the reflection . . . Theory typically uses the assumption that we have too many ethical ideas, some of which may well turn out to be mere prejudices. Our major problem now is actually that we have not too many but too few, and we need to cherish as many as we can.[6]

It is hard to be sure, but Williams seems to be demanding that 'critical reflection' gives us full-blooded things to live for and not merely pallid, highly general reasons for action.

Though there are some normative ethical theories, notably liberal ones, that leave it to particular agents to find things to live for, Williams's demand does not seem to be prompted specifically by them. He is uneasy about moral theory in general. He seems to think there is something in the very nature of a normative ethical theory that makes it unsuitable for suggesting to us how we ought to live. But this is not obviously true of utilitarianism, which suggests a selfless, probably Godless, philanthropic way of life, or of a normative ethical theory distilled from the New Testament. Again, it is unclear what Williams means when he says that moral theory assumes we have too many ethical ideas. It may be that moral theory shows that some ideas we have about how to live are not ideas about living or acting *rightly*, and that an interest in acting or living rightly ought to be given particular weight in any deliberation about how to live. But what is wrong with that? Perhaps, as Williams has been known to suggest in discussing utilitarianism, deferring to what is supposedly right impersonally speaking, can deprive us of projects or activities we feel we have a real stake in. Perhaps. But it is begging the question of what is wrong with moral theory to assert that moral theory must do more than tell us what it is right and wrong to do, impersonally speaking.

Williams is in favour of a kind of critical reflection about ethics that recognizes that we can only detach ourselves within limits from, and so can only justify within limits, our ethical practices (ways of life) and the psychological reactions relevant to them. Difficulties, he says, 'arise from any attempt to see philosophical reflection in ethics as a jump to the universalistic standpoint in search of justification, which is then brought back to everyday practice'.[7] What is wrong with any such process is that in some degree it assumes that 'the reflective agent . . . can make himself independent of the life and character he is examining'.[8] But how serious is this problem? Even if it is out of the question to make oneself completely independent of the life and character one is examining, Williams fails to show that a degree, even a high degree, of detachment is impossible or undesirable. If something one does as agent turns out to have reasons in favour of it from the standpoint of people other than the agent, or even from the point of view of society in general, then, perhaps, so much the *more* reason for doing it. It is this simple intuition rather than some suspect philosophical picture that lies behind universalistic ascent. And it is an intuition Williams does nothing to discredit.

6 PHILOSOPHY AND IMPRACTICALITY

Williams doubts that moral philosophy is of much use in real life; other philosophers doubt that philosophy in general has practical consequences, at any rate direct ones. One spokesman for this point of view, who thinks that it points to an important difference between philosophy and science, is W. Newton-Smith. As he puts it,

> The practical import of philosophy lies in its very impracticality. Because it does not have implications for practical life it can exist as a place in which the tools of ratiocination are honed to their finest. And in this it keeps alive the critical tradition. It inculcates values – explication and defence – the application of which outside philosophy has practical implications.[9]

These remarks take for granted a controversial division of topics into those that lie within and those that lie outside philosophy. Newton-Smith mentions the 'fundamental questions' of truth, beauty, meaning, knowledge, etc.' which are certainly philosophical, and goes on to contrast discussions of these with discussions of 'abortion, euthanasia, socialism, etc.'.[10] I agree that questions that Newton-Smith calls 'fundamental' lie at the centre of philosophy and that the others do not. I deny that the other questions lie outside philosophy, and I deny, too, that a complete list of the 'fundamental questions' would exclude practical ones. The questions 'Which institutions are just?' and even 'How should one live?' are close to the centre of philosophy because moral philosophy is.

Newton-Smith claims that despite the irrelevance to real life of claims in the theory of meaning and other central areas of philosophy, the standards of criticism in force in those areas can be relevant to practice, for the standards can be applied outside philosophy. I am sympathetic to the claim that philosophy exercises such influence as it has through its critical standards; only I disagree with the idea, which I take to be implicit in the passage quoted from Newton-Smith, that philosophy acts as a kind of repair and maintenance department for tools of ratiocination that it loans to people pursuing practical questions in the real world. Arguments in the ordinary public debate about abortion are more likely to be refined by philosophers who participate in the debate and take sides in it than by philosophers who consider patterns of argument in the abstract. Again, it seems unreasonable to assume that 'tools of ratiocination' are confined to devices with a home in philosophy. Why cannot techniques and standards of persuasion borrowed from journalism or advertising be included as well? Newton-Smith is no doubt right to suggest that philosophy affects practice by way of its contribution to the critical tradition, but he perhaps takes too narrow a view of the custodians and instruments of the critical tradition, and he fails to acknowledge the continuity of philosophical with ordinary debate concerning 'abortion, euthanasia, socialism, etc.'.

Newton-Smith's view is narrow in another way, too, for philosophy need not only contribute techniques of reasoning to thinking about practical questions. It need not even confine itself to techniques of reasoning plus normative and meta-ethical theories. Philosophy can be expected to go beyond this and supply theories about the worth of life, theories that rationalize or show to be ill-founded our reluctance to kill, theories that disclose foundations for, or declare groundless, our belief that death is a misfortune. Perhaps surprisingly, the recent growth in literature applying moral theory to life and death issues has not been accompanied by a correspondingly marked interest in the theory of the worth of life.

At least one fragment of an existing normative ethical account, however, provides a basis for work on the worth of life and the disvalue of death. I have in mind the theory, if 'theory' is the right word, of what the American philosopher John Rawls has called the 'primary goods'; such things as health, vigour, intelligence and imagination, as well as goods like liberty, opportunity, wealth, income and self-respect.[11] If, as Rawls claims, these goods advance *any* rational life plan, then they are likely to be among the things that make any rational human life good. A fully developed theory of primary goods might be a further product of philosophy, one to add to normative and meta-ethics. And there may be more. A fully-developed theory of primary goods will not determine which specific life plans are better than others, and yet plainly, identifying good life plans would be one natural function of a substantive theory of worthwhile life. I suggest that philosophy can fill even this gap – with a little outside help. I suggest that in this connection philosophy can join forces with the branch of literature called biography. In an earlier age, accounts of the lives of saints and heroes had a use in showing people how to live virtuously. Accounts of a wider selection of lives, not necessarily those of upright people, could provide the raw material of a theory of worthwhile lives to add to moral theory.

7 EXAGGERATED EXPECTATIONS

I argued earlier that philosophy could have two benefits in the area of life and death. It could help to create tolerance both of dissenting views in debate and of action taken by doctors, nurses and police in difficult circumstances. It could also help to raise standards of justification for the policy decisions of politicians, who might otherwise act successfully as mouthpieces for professional lobbyists. These are benefits, but are they the only benefits that philosophy can be expected to confer? Should philosophy not lead moral debate rather than just take the muddle and intolerance out of it? Or if not lead the debate, should philosophy not decide who wins the debate? The question of whether philosophy should lead the debate has already been partially answered. Since many of the positions in actual moral debate are derived from different philosophical theories, there is a clear sense in which, whether explicitly or not, philosophy does make the running. Of course, once injected into public discussion, positions derived from philosophy may not be promoted there by philosophers: perhaps the question is why *that* is so, why moral philosophers are not principal advocates for views with roots in their subject. The first thing to be said in reply is that it is not true everywhere that philosophers have excused themselves from public debate and withdrawn into the background. Where philosophers in Britain and America have withdrawn they have done so as a result of over-emphasizing meta-ethical questions. Recently the pendulum has swung back and moral philosophers are increasingly discussing, albeit often only among themselves, the issues that the lobbies and interest groups have got hold of.

When philosophers are actively concerned with questions about morality, and about life and death in particular, are they specially suited by their training to decide which of the competing answers ought to prevail? Are the moral views offered by philosophers particularly authoritative? The idea that moral philosophers *are* well qualified to adjudicate, and that their views carry special weight, may help to explain why moral philosophers are sometimes appointed in Britain to advise governments on morally difficult or controversial legislation, and why they sometimes find work in the United States as advisers on morality to large businesses and hospitals, or as agony aunts in high-brow magazines. In any case, the idea that philosophy, or a branch of it, equips people with special moral acuity, is ancient.[12] In the next section I shall give reasons for doubting whether the idea is correct.

8 PHILOSOPHY AND PRIVILEGED ACCESS TO THE GOOD

Plato is perhaps the most famous exponent of the view that true moral knowledge requires a philosophical education.[13] Though he admitted that people of a 'non-philosophical nature' could judge, and often judge correctly, whether a particular person or action was good or just, he doubted that their judgements were well-grounded – informed by acquaintance with a fixed standard of goodness or justice. Indeed, he thought that general ignorance of such standards was evident from the everyday ascription of conflicting evaluative terms such as 'good' and 'bad', 'just' and 'unjust', to the same person or action, viewed from different angles. The few people who were consciously acquainted with a standard of goodness or justice, or who had it in them to become so acquainted, were of a philosophical nature; and they alone could have knowledge of what the good and the just really were. Other, less gifted, beings could at best have true opinion. They were people whose evaluative judgements could change easily under persuasive pressure, and who often experienced difficulty arriving at any definite evaluative judgements in the first place.

One group of people whom Plato meant to include among the unphilosophical were the Sophists, itinerant moral teachers in ancient Greece. For a fee they would instruct wealthy young men how to succeed in practical affairs. Their leading idea was that in order to succeed one had to acquire political power, which depended on being able to win the good opinion of public assemblies by persuasion. Socrates had pioneered the criticism of the Sophists by showing that their techniques, though ostensibly for persuading assemblies that certain actions or policies were good or just, could be applied by speakers who did not know good from evil or just from unjust. That speakers were often ignorant of these distinctions was shown by their inability to say what guided their application of evaluative terms.

That audiences were often ignorant too, was shown by their inability to spot the ungoverned uses of terms like 'good' and 'just', even when Socratic interrogation had *disclosed* that the uses were ungoverned. According to Socrates the beginning of moral wisdom was the realization that one did not know what goodness really was.

Plato's Theory of Forms helped to explain what this not knowing consisted in. According to Book V of the *Republic* it consisted in being acquainted with good things and mistaking those good things for goodness itself. To put it another way, the ignorance of non-philosophical people consisted in judging about the good and the just without a standard of goodness or justice. Plato called this and other standards, such as the standard of truth and the standard of beauty, the 'Forms'. He conceived of Forms as abstract, unchanging objects, outside space and time, accessible to the pure intellect, but out of the reach of ordinary experience. Good things and just acts, which *were* encountered in experience, only gave people inklings of the corresponding Forms. They were mere appearances that the Forms presented. Someone acquainted only with the appearances of the good and the just only happened to tell the good from the bad and the just from the unjust. His correct identifications of certain people as good, for example, showed that he had true opinion, not knowledge. The philosopher, on the other hand, was someone who, after a rigorous intellectual training, would start to see the common feature underlying appearances of the good. He would have the standard lacked by the pre-philosophical person. The process of coming to a closer acquaintance with the Form of the Good was likened by Plato to leaving the dim recesses of a cave and seeing sunlight for the first time. This coming out would crown a philosophical education focused on the mind-sharpening arts of dialectic and geometry.

Plato's account is extremely arresting, but it is also questionable. To begin with, it implies that the true opinion of the non-philosopher and the knowledge of the philosopher are concerned with radically different things, fleeting appearances on the one hand and unchanging abstractions on the other. This is hard to accept. We expect opinion and knowledge about the good and the just to be, in some sense, opinion and knowledge about the same thing. Another problem is that Plato tends to make knowledge of the good too much like knowledge of the underlying structure of a natural substance, like gold. Gold presents a certain characteristic set of appearances which, as it happens, coincide with the characteristic appearance of iron pyrites or fool's gold. If one does not know how to distinguish real gold from fool's gold, then it is in a certain sense lucky if one's identifications of things as gold turn out to be correct. Had iron pyrites been encountered one's identifications would have been exactly the same and quite incorrect. According to Plato the unphilosophical are in a position similar to amateur identifiers of gold. They may identify as good people those who are in fact good, or identify as just actions those that really are just. But since they could easily have been taken in by appearances or by rhetoric and have identified the unjust as just and the bad as good, they are lucky to be right and therefore have only true opinion, not knowledge. To have knowledge, according to Plato, they have to get underneath appearances, just as, to be able to tell real from fool's gold, one has to be able to recognize the underlying physical structure that distinguishes the one substance from the other. This seems to be the wrong model for well-founded moral discernment. It is true that there is a distinction between the apparent and the real in relation to good people and just acts, but grasping this distinction is not a matter of getting underneath experience to some hidden structure, or getting beyond experience to something eternal and unchanging. It is more likely to be a matter of getting *more* experience of different kinds of character and the demands of different situations.

No doubt some people are better than others at recognizing the good or the just. They do not, however, seem to need a special education, let alone a philosophical one. The people in question are those in all walks of life with wisdom or good judgement, people who know how to size up the demands that situations make of them, and, where situations make conflicting demands, which to give the greater weight. They are people who know what value to put on different actions, individuals, policies. They know which ends to pursue and what means to adopt in pursuing them. They are better than most people at evaluations. Do they, however, have something that is properly called 'moral expertise'?

If moral expertise is supposed to be intelligible by analogy with expertise in the recognition of gold, we should expect there to be some necessary and sufficient condition for an action's or a person's counting as good or just, such that a specially trained few are able to recognize the condition as obtaining when it does. But the people we are assuming to qualify as moral experts if any do, namely those who are wise or who have good judgement, are very plausibly said to operate without necessary and sufficient conditions. Their experience acquaints them with particular people, actions and situations, and in reaction to them their judgements and dispositions to act are altered and refined. There is no reason to assume that acquaintance with some general definition of goodness or justice underlies wisdom. Nor is it necessary to suppose that people become wise or acquire good judgement only by special training. Intelligence plus a suitably wide experience of life are sometimes enough.

9 PHILOSOPHY AND MORAL DILEMMAS

The idea that there is such a thing as moral expertise, that this expertise is related to an understanding that goes beyond or underneath experience, and that only philosophers have this understanding, does not turn out to be very persuasive. But Plato's is only one way of exaggerating the contribution that philosophy makes to moral understanding and right conduct. In our own day we have others. There are those in and out of the subject who think that philosophy is of special use in the resolution of concrete dilemmas of medical practice.

In the introduction to his recent book, *The Value of Life*, John Harris argues that philosophy is suited to solving concrete medical ethical problems because of a necessary connection between ethics and reason-giving on the one hand, and, presumably, philosophy and reason-giving on the other. If, Harris says,

> something is right or wrong, morally right or wrong, there must be some reason why this is so . . . Indeed, someone can only claim that actions or decisions stem from moral conviction, or are dictated by moral considerations – are in short part of an attempt to live by ethical standards, if they can say why those actions and decisions are *right*, if they can show how they are *justified*.[14]

Harris goes on to say that moral judgement is always, *inter alia*, a judgement that certain events would make the world better or worse. He claims that such a judgement would be 'incoherent if the maker of that judgement could not say why [the world] would be better or worse in these and these circumstances'.[15] If these claims were correct, ordinary moral judgements and philosophy's justifications for them would indeed be made for one another. In fact, however, Harris's claims are doubtful. Surely someone can live by ethical standards and suffer from an inarticulateness, or enjoy a lack of self-consciousness, that precludes the giving of reasons. Again, in the justification of moral beliefs as in the justification of any other beliefs, reasons eventually run out. Harris implies, but does not explain why, beliefs for which reasons can be given must fail to be moral. I agree with Harris that philosophy can often give reasons for moral beliefs, but not that it always can or that it is of the essence of a moral belief that it be justifiable.

Harris claims that philosophy can help people to resolve, not just understand, ethical dilemmas in medicine, and he explains the power of philosophy to resolve the dilemmas by reference to the traditional philosophical task of justifying our most basic beliefs. Since basic beliefs often have to be reassessed in resolving medical ethical dilemmas, and since philosophy offers means of carrying out this reassessment, philosophy can help with the dilemmas. But even if challenging basic beliefs and values is necessary for confronting the dilemmas of medical ethics, and even if philosophy equips people to do the challenging, it is not obvious that philosophy can help to resolve the dilemmas. This is because many different ethical theories are represented in the subject, not all of them sensitive to the same aspects of the dilemmas up for resolution. In claiming that philosophy can actually resolve medical ethical dilemmas Harris seems to me to ignore the conflicting theoretical approaches that philosophy routinely brings to bear on ethical dilemmas.

The much-discussed conflict between 'rights' theories and utilitarianism in normative ethics is one example of what I have in mind. It underscores the point made earlier that normative ethics is not the name of just one systematic account of the difference between right and wrong. Until methods are found for weighing the claims of competing theories in the same balance and deciding between them, no one piece of practical advice can be expected to come from all normative ethical theories at once. Probably several pieces of advice, each backed by reasons that are good in some normative theory or other, will come forward, each deserving consideration until it can be positively excluded.

In relation to medical practice as in relation to the public debate about medical practice, it seems a mistake to expect philosophy to reduce to one the number of legitimate options, or to identify a uniquely tenable theoretical stance.

On the other hand, it may be in the process of *trying* to reduce to one the number of options or in the process of trying to demonstrate the correctness of a particular position (and conspicuously failing to do so) that a piece of philosophy most effectively alerts us to the existence of alternatives. So while I do not share Harris's confidence that philosophy can actually resolve medical ethical dilemmas, or give conclusive reasons for one moral conviction as against another, I think some value may attach to the attempt to resolve medical ethical dilemmas and the attempt to prove certain moral contentions, by employing ordinary standards of reasoning in philosophy. These standards usually operate to disclose the respects in which a favoured position is not the whole truth; it is these standards that are likely to be philosophy's most valuable contribution to moral knowledge, not some specially authoritative view worked out in keeping with the standards.

NOTES

1 The same goes for guidance about when it is permissible to allow to die. See Harris, John (1985) *The Value of Life: An Introduction to Medical Ethics*, Routledge & Kegan Paul.

2 'Because God commands it' could function as a reason for doing or omitting something, a reason some would regard as a principle. Yet the reason mentions a specific person. Do we not have an exception to the rule that principles be impersonal? Not necessarily, since it is controversial whether it is a complete statement of the reason for the action or omission. These could be something about the action or omission that accounts for God's commanding it, and that independently is a reason for the action or omission, so that the mention of God becomes redundant.

3 For example, it may be doubted whether moral reasons necessarily promote the well-being of others. Perhaps what is necessary is that they be reasons for certain courses of action independently of the agent's wishes or desires. This rather formal way of distinguishing moral from non-moral reasons is derived from Kant. See below, Chapter 3.

4 See Beauchamp, Tom L. and Childress, James F. (1983, 2nd

edn) *Principles of Biomedical Ethics*, Oxford University Press, pp. 9ff. and Appendix II.

5 I am not saying that people are gratuitously persuaded whenever they are moved by rhetoric that appeals to their emotions; my complaint is against rhetoric that trades on emotions involving false or disputable beliefs.

6 Williams, Bernard (1985) *Ethics and the Limits of Philosophy*, Fontana, pp. 116–17.

7 *Ibid.*, p. 110.

8 *Ibid.*

9 Newton-Smith, W., 'The Role of Interests in Science', in Phillips Griffiths, A. (ed.) (1985) *Philosophy and Practice*, Cambridge University Press, p. 73.

10 *Ibid.*, p. 72.

11 Rawls, John (1973) *A Theory of Justice*, Oxford University Press, pp. 62 and 396.

12 A recent collection on euthanasia edited by A. B. Downey and Barbara Smoker contains pieces by philosophers as well as doctors and lawyers. It is subtitled 'Experts debate the right to die'. What are any of these people supposed to be experts about? Medicine and the law and ethical theory, yes. Experts about the rightness and wrongness of euthanasia? Not if what I go on to say is right.

13 Plato, *Republic*, Bk. V.

14 Harris, *op. cit.*, pp. 4–5.

15 *Ibid.*, p. 5.

CHAPTER TWO

A selected controversy

1 APPLYING PHILOSOPHY

Philosophy improves on ordinary moral rhetoric, but not by putting something entirely different in its place. Although arguments given by philosophers can in general be expected to be more precise and more consistent than those put forward in ordinary conversation or in lobbyists' pamphlets, they can be just as partisan and reach the same conclusions. The distinction between a lobbyist's and a philosopher's argument can even disappear. Sometimes a persuasive tract for a wide audience is written by a philosopher, and despite being directed at the general public, it is cited and discussed in philosophical journals.[1] As a rule, however, pieces of persuasive writing for a wide audience do not double as items of philosophical literature. As a rule, lobbyists who make speeches are not trained in methods of analysis and argument. So it may be in relation to these standard speeches and tracts that we will be able to see most clearly the use of the critical standards recognized in philosophy.

Where a question addressed by a speech or tract is a large one and arguments appear weighty on both sides, philosophical resources may be required in order to decide which side to believe; where the arguments on each side only seem weighty but in fact are not, there too, it may be necessary to rely on philosophy if one is to discover as much. Hence the ingredients of this chapter: one large question, a host of arguments for conflicting answers and an indication of how the discussion might be taken further and deeper with the aid of philosophy. The large question is that of the rightness of capital punishment; the conflicting answers are those given by British politicians in speeches during a Parliamentary debate in 1982.

The speeches are going to be considered in the form in which they appear in the official record of the debate. We can assume that in this form they are slightly more polished than they were when actually delivered but considerably *less* polished than they would have been if read out from a text prepared for publication. In other words, even in their official version the speeches have something of the character of spontaneous contributions to a discussion, albeit contributions by people who are used to public speaking and who know in advance what they want to say. In this particular debate, the spontaneity was in fact greater than usual, for MPs were free to break ranks and vote and speak as their consciences, not their political parties, dictated. This meant that the characteristic left/right split of British parliamentary debate was not much in evidence in MPs' speeches.

Perhaps it would be improper to call the speeches 'ordinary moral rhetoric'. Nevertheless they have something in common with ordinary moral rhetoric, for some of the speeches contain quotations from letters and spoken comments received from ordinary constituents, letters and comments intended to persuade, and often endorsed by, the Members of Parliament who conveyed them. Speeches that did not quote directly sometimes purported to describe the views of constituents. To the extent that the speeches represented what the average constituent might have said for or against the death penalty they can be regarded as continuous with ordinary moral rhetoric. Other speeches had something in common with lobbyists' tracts, for they drew arguments and statistics from the publications of organized interest groups. In testing all of these speeches for clarity, consistency and fairness, then, one is indirectly testing ordinary and lobbyists' rhetoric at the same time.

As some of the shortcomings of the speeches emerge, we will get an impression of standard weaknesses in moral rhetoric about life and death issues in general: For example, we will see that speeches in the debate often beg factual questions, notably about the effects on crime of different kinds of penal measures. We will see that statistics are misused. We will see that undue weight is sometimes given to anecdotes and reports of legal cases. We will see that questions about the form of legislation are mixed up with questions about the morality of capital punishment. Finally, we will see that when the moral questions are properly distinguished from the others, MPs' answers to these questions are often incomplete.

2 PLEADING FOR THE DEATH PENALTY

On 11 May 1982, the British House of Commons debated clauses in the Criminal Justice Bill that, if approved, would have reintroduced the death penalty for certain categories of crime in England and Wales. In the debate which had led to the virtual abolition of capital punishment in 1965, the death penalty had been thought too extreme for at least one quite common type of murder, murder committed within the family. One of the clauses debated in 1982 made murder in general liable to capital punishment, but Members of Parliament who voted against it were able to support capital punishment for four other, more specific offences. New clause 19 called for terrorist acts involving the loss of life to be made capital crimes. New clause 20 made murder by fire-arms or explosives punishable by execution. New clause 21 specified death as the maximum penalty for the murder of police and prison officers. Finally, new clause 27 proposed to introduce capital punishment for murder in the course of burglary or robbery involving the use of offensive weapons.

Deterrence

Vivian Bendall tabled all five clauses and opened the debate.[2] Speaking first to the catch-all clause concerning murder, he said that the

> death penalty would act as a deterrent. A would-be murderer will think twice before taking a life if he knows that he may

> well forfeit his own in so doing. If one examines the homicides that have been reported to the police since 1964, the year the death penalty was done away with on a trial basis, one sees that the figure for murders in 1964 was 296. In 1980, the figure was 620. The number has more than doubled. (p. 319, col. 610)

Later in his speech Bendall gave statistics for murders of police officers. 'In the seventeen years prior to the death penalty being abolished', he said, 'eleven police officers were murdered. In the seventeen years since the death penalty was abolished, twenty-seven have been murdered. That is another doubling of the figure. The figures speak for themselves' (p. 320, col. 612).

Do the figures speak for themselves? The fact that murders increased after the abolition of the death penalty does not show that murders increased *because* of the abolition of the death penalty. But unless this causal claim is demonstrated, it is hard to show that the death penalty would prevent murder or reduce the numbers of murders. Bendall also made questionable use of his figures for police killings. He compared the seventeen-year period before abolition to the seventeen-year period after abolition, and found at the end of the second period a doubling of the figure at the end of the first. Indeed, the figure *more* than doubled. But the fact that it did has to be taken together with another: that on average fewer than two police officers per year were murdered in either seventeen-year period. Bendall's method of accounting made the trend appear more alarming than it had to.

The increase in the number of murders *was* evidence for Bendall's claim that the abolition of the death penalty encouraged an increase in the rate of homicide. The point is, it was weak evidence: other things besides the abolition of the death penalty could have led to more murders, for example a growing belief, independent of the penalty, that the rate of successful detection of murder was going down. Or, to cite a very different possibility, if many murders were due to tensions within families, then an increase in factors creating such tensions, factors as diverse as adultery and unemployment, could have increased the murder rate.

Nothing in Bendall's speech excluded these rival explanations of his figures.

Other Members of Parliament who regretted the earlier abolition of the death penalty failed, as Bendall did, to demonstrate a causal connection between abolition and subsequent rates of crime. But even if this *had* been demonstrated, it would have remained to show that by re-introducing capital punishment potential murderers would have been deterred. The claim that people can be deterred from doing a thing by such and such a measure is the claim that such and such a measure can take away or weaken the motivation people have for doing the thing. What did Bendall and other like-minded politicians do to show that the death penalty would weaken the many different kinds of motivation people have for murder? There is Bendall's initial claim that someone who knew he could well forfeit his life for murder would think twice about committing it. A potential murderer, according to this line of thought, would not risk losing his own life. A *rational* murderer might not risk it if he thought the matter over. But that leaves out people who murder in a fit of passion, or those who plan to take away the lives of others *and* their own. Many murders in Britain fall into the latter two categories, according to statistics covering the period from 1957 to 1972, prepared with the help of the Home Office.[3]

The matter of motivation was considered briefly in Bendall's speech after an intervention by another MP. Harry Greenway came in after Bendall had given statistics concerning the use of firearms and explosives in crimes committed in England and Wales in the 1970s.

> *Mr Bendall* ... The use of firearms and explosives must be stopped. If innocent people are otherwise to be maimed and killed, the only deterrent and the only answer is the return of the death penalty.
>
> *Mr Harry Greenway* (Ealing, North) Will my hon. Friend go behind the important statistics that he is giving to the House and explain what motivates men and women to use firearms and therefore commit the murders that he has described.

> *Mr Bendall* Many people commit crimes. With regard to terrorism, the motive is obviously political. With regard to armed robbery, I firmly believe that those concerned arm themselves because they believe that by shooting themselves out of trouble they may not be caught. (p. 320, cols. 611–12)

Perhaps Bendall is right about armed robbers. Perhaps they do take arms to shoot their way out of trouble. Then again, they may take arms to frighten people into co-operating with them, never intending to fire a shot. Nothing in Bendall's speech excludes the second possibility. As for the political motive for terrorism, what did Bendall do to show that the death penalty takes away or weakens this motive? At one point he said, 'I believe that relatives would be able to persuade potential murderers to adopt methods other than senseless and barbaric acts of terrorism if the death penalty were reintroduced' (p. 319, col. 620). But would not relatives have a strong incentive for dissuading terrorists if the penalty were life imprisonment rather than death?

In fact, it is extremely difficult to demonstrate that capital punishment deters, or that it deters more effectively than long periods of imprisonment. A recent American review of the major studies in the area concludes that 'the deterrent effect of capital punishment is definitely not a settled matter' and that the statistical methods necessary for reaching firm conclusions have yet to be devised.[4] A number of speakers in the Parliamentary debate pointed out the inconclusiveness of the relevant research but failed to sway those who believed, for reasons of their own, that the death penalty *was* a deterrent. For example, in replying to Robert Kilroy-Silk, who said that evidence of the deterrent effect was not compelling, one of the advocates of the death penalty, Teddy Taylor, cited figures showing a jump in the rate of reported homicides after the abolition of capital punishment in England and Wales. Taylor gave further figures showing a rise in the rate of convictions for murder in Scotland after abolition. But this is another instance of the question-begging form of argument we earlier saw being employed by Bendall. Taylor remarked in passing that 'the fact that the hon. Member for Ormskirk [Kilroy-Silk] believes that the number of murders has not increased, and that capital punishment does not deter, does not mean that that is true' (p. 327, col. 625). The same could be said of the blank assertion that capital punishment *does* deter and that the number of murders goes up as a result of abolition.

At least two speakers in the debate gave evidence of a deterrent effect for capital punishment based on the testimony of people who claimed to have been put off themselves. One of the two speakers, Arthur Lewis, had once opposed capital punishment. Now he had changed his mind for

> many reasons. One reason that has stuck in my mind, and which has been proved to me beyond question, is that there was once a professional burglar in the constituency who consistently boasted of the fact that he had spent about one-third of his life in prison . . . He said to me 'I am a professional burglar. Before we go out on a job we plan it down to every detail. Before we go into the boozer to have a drink we say "Don't forget, no shooters" – shooters being guns. He added 'We did our job and didn't have shooters because at that time there was capital punishment. Our wives, girlfriends and our mums said "Whatever you do, do not carry a shooter because if you are caught you might be topped". If you do away with capital punishment they will all be carrying shooters.' (pp. 344–5, cols. 660–1)

Arthur Lewis went on to report his 'friend' as saying that where the penalty for robbery with and robbery without fire-arms was the same, it increased the chances of 'getting away with it' to carry sawn-off shotguns. Here, according to Lewis, was good evidence of the deterrent effect of capital punishment.

Lewis's report of the burglar's views is, I think, credible and persuasive. It shows that capital punishment at some time deterred some people, perhaps a large number of professional burglars, from going armed. The question is how good an argument for capital punishment this particular deterrent effect is. Lewis's friend's story concerns homicide in the course of robbery and suggests that this crime can be discouraged if it is capitally punishable. Its lesson for other sorts of crime is unclear. And if it is authoritative about the psychological reactions of anyone, it is so only for the professional thief, not the casual robber or the terrorist or the young, violence-loving thug. So it is unclear what it shows. *Perhaps* it justifies a vote in favour of Bendall's clause 27, making death a possible penalty for robbery involving the use of fire-arms. Even this is uncertain, because it may not be true that most intending robbers are influenced by the considerations that weighed with Lewis's 'friend'.

Another supporter of the reintroduction of capital punishment in the House of Commons debate was Malcolm Thornton. He also spoke up for the deterrent effect of capital punishment, but confessed that he believed that the arguments were 'marginal' on either side. He explained his own position like this:

> [It] is important that hon. Members say why they are prepared to support a course of action. I go back to the occasion when, as a very young man, I talked to a prison chaplain who had officiated at the executions of three murderers. He talked about not only his own experiences but the experiences of some of his colleagues. Between them they had officiated at the executions of eleven murderers . . . He said many things, but one thing especially stuck in my mind and I can recall his words to this day. He said that when a man is taken to be hanged it is an especially horrible experience. He is seldom able to walk and is usually dragged. He is out of control. He is vomiting with fear and unable to control his bowels. The prison chaplain said, 'It is an experience we all found extremely degrading – an experience which because we were there on behalf of society, must inevitably degrade society as well. But do not ever, ever underestimate the deterrent effect of this most awful punishment.' The thought of being hanged by the neck until one is dead, which we all know is an extremely clinical way of despatching someone, would certainly act as a deterrent to me. It should be available to the courts and the vast majority of our fellow citizens believe in it. For that reason, I shall go . . . and vote for the new clauses. (p. 349, col. 670)

The testimony of the prison chaplain as reported by Thornton is certainly compelling; but does it not amount to an argument *against* capital punishment, on the ground that it degrades society? True, the chaplain attested to the deterrent effect of hanging. But it is unclear that this outweighed or cancelled out the terrible effects on the man being punished and the people officiating.

Giving the public what they want

The deterrent effect of capital punishment was not the only ground offered for its reintroduction in the new clauses of the Criminal Justice Bill. Vivian Bendall, concluding the opening speech in the debate, cited then recent soundings of public opinion:

> In the 1975 opinion poll, sixty-four per cent favoured capital punishment. In the 1981 Gallup poll, the figure was sixty-nine per cent; and in the Gallup poll just a few weeks ago seventy-eight per cent, seventy-five per cent and seventy-four per cent favoured the death penalty for certain categories of murder. The Police Federation has received more than 200,000 signatures in favour of capital punishment and I suspect that many hon. Members have received letters supporting it. In the correspondence that I have received, the ratio is 30:1 in favour. Moreover, I have today received a petition from the Manchester and Merseyside areas, with 125,000 signatures, seeking a binding referendum on the question of capital punishment. (p. 321, col. 614)

He went on to suggest that a vote for the return of capital punishment was 'needed if democracy was to be upheld'.

Suppose the opinion polls that Bendall cited were accurate and that three-quarters of the British people were in favour of capital punishment. Does the fact that a majority supports it make the death penalty right? Does the fact that a majority supports it mean that a vote by an MP against capital punishment is anti-democratic? Several speakers gave reasons for answering 'No' to the second question. One of these was Edward Heath, who quoted Edmund Burke on the duty of a representative of the people: 'Your representative owes you, not his industry only, but his judgement; and he betrays instead of serving you if he sacrifices it to your opinion.' For Heath, it was the duty of a democratically elected representative not to act as a mere mouthpiece for his constituents, but to vote as his own conscience or judgement directed. Others agreed with Heath. 'We are representatives,' said Robert Kilroy-Silk, 'not delegates' (p. 327, col. 625).[5]

Neither Kilroy-Silk nor Heath went so far as to say that the overwhelming popular support for capital punishment was unjustified, or founded on a misconception. In an assembly made up of people who are elected by majorities, it is hard to call into question the correctness of opinions of majorities without undercutting one's own legitimacy. Still, the fact that it is awkward to query majority views does not mean that they are beyond criticism. The view that capital punishment ought to be reintroduced, if it *is* the view of a majority, is no exception. If we are to accept it as correct, it is not enough to be told that everyone else accepts it or that the overwhelming majority do: there should be some independent ground of its correctness which explains why everyone or most people accept it. This independent ground is precisely what is left out of Bendall's list of opinion-poll results.

The same omission was made by Teddy Taylor in the Parliamentary debate when he attempted to answer the view of Heath and Kilroy-Silk that MPs were not bound to vote as their constituents would have done. Taylor said:

> We will make a great mistake if we consider public opinion on this issue in the same way as we consider public opinion on issues that can be determined at general elections. Every five years people can decide about the running of the economy and so on. They have a choice. Therefore, it is fair and reasonable too that hon. Members should exercise their judgement on such issues as they arise. However . . . the situation is different if people cannot decide on an issue every five years and if the politicians of the majority parties tend to be drawn from a group with one consistent point of view while the majority hold a different view. (p. 327, col. 626)

This is to regret majority support in Parliament for views different from those of the majority of the electorate at large: it is not to give a reason why the views of the larger majority are right.

Must there be a reason to think that a majority opinion is right before it is incorporated into the law of a democratic state? This is the large question hovering behind the exchanges between Bendall and Heath, between Kilroy-Silk and Taylor. It is possible to hold that in a democracy the laws should reflect the views of the majority right *or* wrong. But it seems to me that whether this position is reasonable depends on what the views of the majority are about, and also on the purpose of a liberal democracy. If a liberal democracy exists to enable each of the many to pursue his own ends, and exists also to promote positively the ends most of the many share, then the fact that many people in a democracy want a particular thing is by itself a strong argument for legislating in favour of it. In particular, if the assumptions about ends just outlined are accepted, majority support for capital punishment would be a strong argument for legislating in favour of it.

But at this point it is important to distinguish between ways in which something can be wanted. It is possible to want capital punishment for murder as a means of getting something else that is desirable, say a situation in which there are fewer murders. It is also possible to want capital punishment for murder and want it for its own sake, for example in the belief that that crime and that punishment are made for one another. Now if capital punishment for murder were wanted for its own sake by many people in a democracy, a good case would exist for making it legal, at any rate on present assumptions. On the other hand, if capital punishment for murder were desired for its supposed power of reducing the number of murders, and it actually had no such effect, or it was doubtful that it had such an effect, then the argument in favour of capital punishment legislation would be weak. Similarly if capital punishment *did* have the desired effect but the means of inflicting the death penalty were found extremely repellent by most people. At best there would be an argument for legislating in favour of whatever palatable measures in fact reduced the rate of murder. And that leaves completely unspecified the content of the legislation.

Now as might already have been gathered from the parts of their speeches quoted earlier, and as will become clearer in the next section, Bendall and Taylor favoured capital punishment only as a means of reducing violent crime, and both took their view to mirror that of a majority outside Parliament. If they were right and the majority wanted capital punishment only as a means to something else, then *no* particular authority attaches to the majority view. The majority view is only acceptable, is only legitimately translated into law, if the evidence shows that capital punishment does in fact reduce the rate of violent crime. Beliefs about means to ends are beliefs about what will produce certain effects and no beliefs about what will produce certain effects are infallible, even if a majority subscribes to them. I have admitted that on present assumptions about the purpose of democracy there is a good case for introducing capital punishment for murder, where the many want it for its own sake. But even this sort of shared desire seems to have limited authority, since it is a good reason for not giving the majority what they want that what they want is evil, and since it is conceivable that some desires of a majority can be just that: evil.

Revenge and the saving of life

A number of speakers, both opponents and supporters of the return of capital punishment, said that they were opposed to revenge. Opponents of capital punishment claimed that in administering the death penalty society was acting out of revenge. Supporters, on the other hand, argued that capital punishment was not revenge but something else. Teddy Taylor again:

> Those who support capital punishment do not want to kill more people, but we genuinely believe – and the evidence supports our view – that it would lead to the saving of innocent life. I am sure that few of us . . . who vote for the clauses tonight will do so because we believe in revenge or because we think it is an appropriate penalty. We do so only because the evidence shows . . . that if we had such a deterrent we would save innocent human lives. (pp. 327–8, cols. 626–7)

Apparently, Taylor's idea was that with capital punishment to put them off, some would-be murderers would not kill;

as a result the lives of their would-be victims would not be lost. The saving of would-be victims' lives, not a need to make convicted criminals pay for actual victims' lives, was supposed to justify capital punishment. But it is hard to adduce evidence for the claim that if not for capital punishment so and so many lives would have been lost.

Difficult as it is to verify, Taylor's claim is at least more cogently formulated than the view of a fellow supporter of capital punishment in the 1982 debate, Jill Knight. 'The only reason why I support the new clause 22 and making the sentence of capital punishment available to the courts is that I want to save life. I am not interested in the least in revenge' (p. 352, col. 676). But it could not be life full-stop she wanted to save if she was in favour of taking the lives of murderers. It had to be victims' lives or innocent lives. Again, instead of estimating the number of lives that would be saved through the deterrent effect of the death penalty, Knight dwelt on the 'large and frightening number of known murderers who have been convicted, sent to prison and let out and who have killed again'. These cases do not tell in favour of the death penalty as a deterrent to others but, rather, underline the fact that it is the most effective kind of incapacitation. What is more, the cases do not show that capital punishment is the right treatment for convicted murderers but (at best) that release from prison is the wrong treatment.

In their eagerness to dissociate themselves from those who would support killing in revenge, Taylor, Knight and a number of other speakers in the debate seemed reluctant to claim that death was justly deserved for murder. Taylor, indeed, expressly disowned the idea that capital punishment was the 'appropriate' penalty. Perhaps, like some who spoke against capital punishment, Taylor and Knight saw little difference between a 'just desert' view and support for revenge. Nevertheless, there *is* a difference, one that is brought out in other speeches made in the debate. Consider the following exchange between Edward Heath and Percy Grieve.

Mr Heath The real point which is emphasized to me by many constituents is that even if the death penalty is not a deterrent, murderers deserve to die. This is the question of revenge. Again, this will be a matter of moral judgement for each of us. I do not believe in revenge. If I were to become the victim of terrorists, I would not wish them to be hanged or killed in any other way for revenge. All that would do is deepen the bitterness which already tragically exists in the conflicts we experience in society, particularly in Northern Ireland.

Mr Percy Grieve (Solihull) My right hon. Friend characterized the demand for the taking of life upon the taking of a life as revenge. May it not be said that society shows its respect for human life by exacting the death penalty against those who have deliberately taken life?

Mr Heath My hon. and learned Friend is right in saying that that is a point of view which can be put forward. It is not one which I share. (p. 324, col. 620)

Heath did not say why he rejected the view. Perhaps, as his remarks before Grieve's intervention suggest, he thought the consequences of exacting the death penalty were worse than the consequences of letting live, even when by exacting the penalty one was marking one's respect for life taken away.

Heath was nevertheless wrong to insinuate that it is only out of revenge that people want murderers to receive the death penalty. Not only is it conceivable that the death penalty is expressive of respect for life wrongly taken away; there is also, and again contrary to Heath, a difference between the simple desire for revenge and the retributivist belief that murderers deserve to die. To name just one consideration, the desire and the belief differ in scope. For, consider: it is not possible to want revenge for the murder of someone whom one was indifferent to, or wanted to see dead oneself. Revenge is always revenge for some supposed injury to oneself or to those one cares about. Take away the appropriate sympathies and the concept of revenge becomes inapplicable. This is not so with the belief that murderers deserve to die. This belief can coherently extend to murderers of people everyone hates or is indifferent to.

There is another difference between giving the offender what he deserves and getting revenge. While both, let us say, involve inflicting pain in return for pain, the two diverge in their scruples about the amount of pain to be returned. To give someone his just desert is to inflict pain equal or proportional to his offence. Revenge, however, is still revenge when the pain inflicted on the offender far exceeds that originally inflicted. *Lex talionis* – the rule of exacting an eye for an eye, a tooth for a tooth – gets its point from the fact that it limits what can be done in return for an offence. It does not allow the pain inflicted to vary with the appetite for pain on the part of the people inflicting it. This suggests a third difference, which is that it is possible to characterize conditions of just desert, but not revenge, without reference to the gratification of appetite.

So defenders of capital punishment might have invoked a straight retributivist defence of capital punishment, i.e. a defence of capital punishment as a means of paying back murderers to the extent they deserved it, without inviting the objection that they were urging revenge. As it was, the argument for deterrence tended to be the dominant one, and for the reasons already given, it was less than conclusive.

3 ARGUMENTS AGAINST CAPITAL PUNISHMENT

Opponents of capital punishment in the Parliamentary debate did not always speak to the moral issues at stake. At times they took up the specific clauses proposed and tried to show that they were inadequate as possible items of new law.

Classifying relevant crimes

William Whitelaw, Home Secretary at the time of the debate and the minister who would have been responsible for putting the reintroduction of capital punishment into effect, commented on the difficulty of deciding which crimes should be made capital offences.

> Very few of those who might support the principle of the death penalty would, I suspect, support its application to all types of murder in all the circumstances in which the offence is committed. A substantial proportion of convictions for murder arise from domestic incidents, and there is, I think, a widely shared feeling that such killings ought not to attract the death penalty.
>
> I take that as just one example of an attempt to draw a dividing line between more and less heinous types of murder to determine which offences ought, or ought not, to attract the death penalty. This would make liable for execution the burglar who, in a panic, strikes out at the householder who disturbs him and then finds that he has killed him, but would absolve from the death penalty the man who deliberately over a period of time slowly poisons his wife to death. Would this distinction be right and just? (p. 331, col. 633)

Other speakers gave further examples of murders that, under the terms of the new clauses, would be treated more leniently than others without necessarily being the less heinous. Since the examples do not so much tell against capital punishment as against a given choice of offences for which capital punishment is made available, I shall not go through them in any detail.

A number of participants in the debate gave reasons for thinking that it would serve no useful purpose to bring terrorism under the death penalty. The penalty would make it easy for those who were determined to appear as martyrs to get their way. Another objection was that, in ear-marking terrorist offences for the death penalty, Parliament would in effect be introducing an unwanted category of political crime. Murder by shooting, initially another plausible category of capitally punishable crime, was objected to on the ground that guns were often used by the mentally unstable or by the sane in moments of high passion. In neither case would the death penalty act as a deterrent. And so on through the different categories of crime.

Reluctant juries and unsafe convictions

Would juries who had it in their power to find people guilty in capital cases actually do so, in view of the seriousness of the death penalty? A number of MPs who spoke against the reinstatement of capital punishment were sceptical. Some forecast that convictions would rest on majority verdicts rather than unanimous verdicts. A verdict of guilty brought in by a majority of jurors only, would show that there was room for doubt, and would call into question the appropriateness of the death sentence in that case.

Other speakers, without predicting that juries would be reluctant to convict, gave reasons why such reluctance would be justified. William Whitelaw noted that 'execution following mistaken conviction is irreversible. No system can guarantee to avoid mistaken conviction' (p. 332, col. 636). Alexander Lyon, making the same general point, gave the details of a case of which he had personal knowledge:

> I cite one case from my own experience as a Minister – the Confait case, in which three youths in Lewisham were convicted of murder. I was asked to intervene because the Court of Appeal had rejected their appeals. The Home Secretary intervenes only when there is new evidence that was not available to the Court, because to overrule the Court would seem an excessive use of prerogative. I breached the principle on that occasion – the one and only such case known to me in English legal history – and sent the case back to the Court of Appeal. I was persuaded that the case had not been properly put to the jury, but I could find no new evidence that would allow me to exercise the power of the prerogative in the normal way.
>
> The Court of Appeal quashed the conviction . . . Mr Justice Fisher, although he was no longer a judge, was asked to conduct an enquiry . . . [H]e took the view that the men had been wrongly convicted of murder, but that they were present at the scene and were probably guilty of arson.
>
> A year or so later, after the conviction had been quashed, two men – one of whom confessed – said that they had been present, had started the fire and had killed the man. (p. 338, cols. 647–8)

In the example given by Lyon at least one of those convicted was old enough to have been eligible for the death penalty. No one convicted in the Confait case was, in fact, hanged, but in other cases wrongful conviction is widely thought to have led to the execution of the innocent. In 1950, Timothy Evans was executed for the murder of his young daughter, although in the course of his trial he had accused another man, John Christie, of the murder of both his daughter and his wife. Christie was subsequently found to have murdered at least six women, four after sexual assault on them. He admitted after Evans's trial to the murder of Evans's wife and daughter. An enquiry that led to Evans's posthumous pardon pronounced that Christie, not Evans, had probably killed the daughter.[6]

At least one supporter of capital punishment was prepared to back the reintroduction of the death penalty while conceding that innocent people are sometimes wrongly executed for capital crimes. J. F. Pawsey said:

> We must have a balance sheet with, on the one hand, the loss of one or perhaps two innocent lives through judicial procedure, and, on the other, the loss of innocent lives by acts of murder that would have been prevented had an effective deterrent been in existence. The balance sheet of life would show that many more people would be alive today if capital punishment had been retained. (p. 330, col. 675)

It is sometimes said that the taking of innocent life is never justifiable. Pawsey denied this. According to him it was sometimes justifiable, justifiable if the number of innocent lives saved by capital punishment was greater than the number lost through wrongful conviction and execution. Pawsey did not defend this line of thought against the charge made by among others John Maxton that 'if we allow one innocent person to be executed, morally we are committing the same, or, in some ways, a worse crime than the person who committed the murder' (p. 340, col. 651). Pawsey might have replied by noting that while murder is always done with the *intention* that death should befall a person who is innocent, no such intention is present in the case of wrongful capital punishment. But this answer to Maxton, though it succeeds in showing that capital punishment in error is not the same as murder, does not justify taking the risk that the innocent will be mistakenly killed by execution. On the contrary, as will emerge later on in this book, it is a question whether anything can justify this risk.

Sanctity of life, brutalization and civilized societies

The moral arguments brought against the reintroduction of capital punishment in the House of Commons debate were to do on the one hand with the risk of executing the wrongfully convicted and, on the other, with what many speakers referred to as the brutal, decadent, 'macabre and corrupting' act of judicial killing. Sometimes arguments of this second kind came close to asserting the principle of the sanctity of life, only to retreat to a more qualified position. Thus Roy Hattersley started out by saying, 'I believe it is morally wrong for the state to execute a man or woman, whatever crime that man or woman may have committed' (p. 333, col. 637). This belief might have been defended with the principle that it is never right to take human life. But, in fact, Hattersley went on immediately to say, 'There are occasions when the state possesses the right, indeed the duty, to take life' as when it acts 'to prevent a terrorist from taking and jeopardizing another life'. However, the state does not have the right to take life, Hattersley said, when it has captured a criminal and has kept him or her in custody. Presumably the act of killing, once the criminal had been captured, struck Hattersley as gratuitous and therefore as abhorrent. He rejected as unproven the proposition that the death penalty would discourage crime, and he dismissed as morally indefensible the policy of executing one man to deter another (p. 333, col. 638).

He also mentioned what he called the 'catastrophes' that would flow from the reintroduction of capital punishment. 'The catastrophes', he said, 'would range from the hanging of the wrong man to the brutalization of society.' We have already noted the risk of executing the innocent. What did Hattersley think would count as brutalization?

> If Members are sceptical about what I call the brutalization of society, let them consider the way in which some newspapers have prepared us for today's debate. Three weeks ago the *News of the World* had Ruth Ellis's daughter supporting capital punishment with a photograph in which she was dressed up and made to look like her executed mother. In the same issue of the *News of the World*, a superannuated hangman described, with the aid of drawings, how sentence is carried out. A return to such a system would inevitably have an effect on the nature and quality of society. The feeling would be spread abroad that in some circumstances the taking of life was justifiable. This would be so no matter what form of judicial execution was introduced. (p. 335, col. 642)

But Hattersley had himself already endorsed the feeling which he feared would be spread abroad. He had earlier said that in some circumstances the state not only had the right but the duty to take human life.

Sometimes what is meant by 'brutalization' in connection with capital punishment is the process by which the public becomes hardened to execution, loses its natural revulsion for hanging, even comes to look upon it as a source of entertainment or as an object of grisly fascination. In the debate Clinton Davis recalled how when he was an

> articled clerk my firm was engaged in the Ruth Ellis case . . . It was a ghoulish situation indeed. I never want to see a situation recur where people wait outside gates for the notice to be posted, for the bell to toll, waiting to see some signification that the prisoner's life has been taken. I do not want to see that situation occur again because it is not the sign of a civilized society. (p. 350, col. 672)

Ruth Ellis was convicted in the 1950s for the murder of a man who had at one time been her lover. The decision to sentence her to death was unpopular, and hastened the abolition of capital punishment. No one who mentioned her case in order to illustrate the brutalizing effects of capital punishment went very far toward showing that its reintroduction would make ghoulish behaviour more prevalent.[7] Instead, several speakers dwelt on the clinical, heartless aspect of the execution. At least one person stressed the unfairness of making anyone play the role of executioner.

Clinton Davis said that he did not want to see repeated what he had witnessed at the time of the execution of Ruth Ellis. He said that he did not want that sort of situation to arise again 'because it is not the sign of a civilized society'. Could an argument against the death penalty be based on the idea of civilization rather than on brutalization? Davis did not sketch such an argument, but it exists in the philosophical literature. A recent version of it, stated by an American philosopher called Jeffrey Reiman,[8] attempts to show that for the same reasons it is good to abolish torture as a punishment for serious crime it is good to shun the death penalty. When torture is abolished in a society there is a reduction in the number of 'horrible things [done] to our fellows' and such a reduction is 'an advance in civilization as long as our lives are not really made more dangerous'.[9] Now Reiman thinks that there is a duty to do what will advance civilization. He thinks that states have a civilizing mission, and he argues that in view of the pain involved in inflicting the death penalty, in view of the unsavouriness of asking anyone to inflict it and the inconclusiveness of arguments for its deterrent effect, abolishing the death penalty would be in the interest of civilization.

This argument should not be dismissed lightly, and in Chapter Five I shall consider a similar line of thought in some detail. For the moment I want to call attention to two disputable premises in Reiman's version of the argument. The first is that capital punishment is one of the 'horrible things' people do to one another. Reiman himself is impatient with the argument that capital punishment does the same wrong to murderers as they do to their victims.[10] He is rightly impatient, for while it is wrong or 'horrible' to kill the innocent, it may not be wrong, or at least not wrong for the same reasons, to kill those who are guilty of murder. Yet the argument from the 'same wrong' seems to be echoed in the idea that a horrible thing is done to the murderer when his life is taken away. Either that, or Reiman questionably assumes that execution is unduly painful. It is a severe punishment, yes, but perhaps not too severe for the serious crime it is applied to. A second disputable premise in

Reiman's argument is that states have a 'civilizing mission', that is, a mission actively to improve citizens by taming their baser impulses. It is possible to argue cogently for a state that does little more than keep people secure from physical attack and their property safe from damage or theft.[11]

Even with its disputable premises Reiman's argument identifies some moral and political principles available to the abolitionist that were either ignored or left inexplicit in the Parliamentary debate. In the debate, the arguments against the reintroduction of capital punishment were not very robust, but in the opinion of most MPs they did not have to be: the burden lay on those who wanted a return to the death penalty to make *their* case.

4 THE LIMITATIONS OF RHETORIC AGAIN

Who won the debate? In one clear sense those opposed to the reintroduction of capital punishment did. They were in the majority, sometimes in the overwhelming majority, when the votes on Bendall's clauses were taken. But did they have the better arguments? It is not clear that they did. Instead, the position seems to be that the other side were unequal to proving their case and that the onus was on them to do so. Overall, and as a number of contributors to the debate remarked, neither side's view was clearly the more compelling. Why was this?

An answer proposed by several speakers was that the issue of capital punishment was primarily a moral one, and that the moral arguments on the two sides were evenly balanced. Jill Knight said, 'Every point on this subject has a counter-balancing argument' (p. 353, col. 677). William Whitelaw took a similar view, counting himself among those who thought that 'the moral and ethical arguments either way cancel out' (p. 330, col. 632). Whitelaw had in mind arguments for two opposing views in particular, one

> that those who kill unlawfully and deliberately automatically forfeit their right to life, and judicial execution is, therefore, just retribution. On the other side are those whose belief in

> the sanctity of life leads them to the unshakeable view that to take life as a judicial act is wrong in itself and contrary to the moral standards on which the law of society should be founded. (p. 330, col. 632)

In fact, however, the first of these positions was not very prominent in the debate, and the second, as far as I have been able to discover, had only a single spokesman. The best-discussed argument, about deterrence, was not always explicitly a moral argument, and the opposed moral arguments that did feature in the debate did not seem to engage one another.

The reason I say that the argument about deterrence was not always explicitly moral is that it was sometimes concerned merely with whether capital punishment had or had not such and such effects on the rate of murder and other violent crime. The arguments were not about whether capital punishment was right when it had the deterrent effect claimed for it. Some speakers, it is true, did mention a ground for the rightness of capital punishment, namely its promise of saving innocent life, but another ground was sometimes assumed. This was to do with the general public's *distress* at the rise in crime, and in particular, violent crime. It was because the deterrent effect of capital punishment was supposed to help reverse the trend and therefore ease the public's distress, that it was supposed to be morally right.

Is the fact that *X* would alleviate public distress a compelling justification for doing *X*? A reasonable answer to the question is that it all depends. If the distress is mild or temporary, or if its intensity is due to some misconception or error, then there could be insufficient reason for alleviating such distress. Again, it could be that the distress is intense and not due in any way to error, and yet the action it would take to alleviate this distress is one that there are good reasons against doing. A complete defence of the deterrence argument for capital punishment would have to show that the death penalty did not relieve questionable kinds of distress, and that it was not itself too awful a means of relieving legitimate distress. It would have to show, for example, that public disquiet at violent crime was severe enough to justify the irreversible penalty of death rather than life imprisonment. It would have to show, again, that the reasons against killing in general were not strong enough to prohibit the relief of public distress by killing. Though it is not easy to show these things, opponents of the deterrence view in the Parliamentary debate did little to exploit these gaps in the deterrence case. Instead, they put forward positions of their own along quite different lines, in their turn often inadequately defended. One speaker, it may be remembered, asserted that it was wrong for the state to execute a man or woman for any crime. Yet little was done to explain why it was wrong if the man or woman was a convicted murderer. Brutalization was mentioned as an undesirable effect of capital punishment, but quite what it was supposed to consist in was left obscure. And it was unclear whether the assertion that it was wrong to execute people or that doing so brutalized society, was intended as an answer to the argument about deterrence, or was meant simply to shift the ground of the debate.

How far were these omissions and unclarities anticipated in our discussion of the shortcomings of moral rhetoric in the last chapter? The unclear terminology of moral rhetoric was one thing cited. So was the problem of getting conflicting positions to engage one another or to render opposed considerations mutually commensurable. Both problems have been illustrated in excerpts from the Parliamentary debate, the former in obvious ways, the latter in the failure of those opposed to capital punishment to express their views in the terms (the relief of public distress) used by the proponents of capital punishment. Two other problems with moral rhetoric were also mentioned in the last chapter: those of narrowness and shallowness of justification. Were these reflected in MPs' speeches? We have already seen evidence of shallowness of justification, especially in connection with the deterrence argument. As for narrowness, only one speaker laid any stress on the parallel between capital punishment and other moral issues.[12] In the next chapter we shall see that philosophy goes some way toward solving these problems, problems of justification in particular.

NOTES

1 See Anscombe, Elizabeth 'Mr Truman's Degree', in her (1981) *Collected Philosophical Papers Volume III: Ethics, Religion and Politics*, Blackwell, pp. 62–71; first published as part of a pamphlet in 1957.

2 All references are by page and column number to *Parliamentary Debates (Hansard)*, fifth series, vol. 23, issue 1243, House of Commons, 11 May 1982, HMSO.

3 *Murder and Capital Punishment in England and Wales*; a pamphlet published in 1979 by the Howard League for Penal Reform and the National Campaign for the Abolition of Capital Punishment.

4 Klein, L., Forst, B. and Filatov, V., 'The Deterrent Effect of Capital Punishment: An Assessment of the Estimates', in Blumstein, A., Cohen, J. and Nagin, D., (eds) (1978) *Deterrence and Incapacitation: Estimating the Effects of Criminal Sanctions on Crime Rates*, National Academy of Sciences, pp. 336–61.

5 In the London *Observer* newspaper for Sunday, 4 January 1987, the MP Julian Critchley had essentially the same reply to a letter he quoted from the organizer of RECAP, a lobby in favour of reintroducing capital punishment. The letter asked Critchley, who had voted against reintroducing capital punishment, whether he had ever polled his supporters on the question of hanging, and whether he had any authority to vote against its reintroduction.

6 Evans, however, was found by the enquiry to have been the probable murderer of his wife. He had not been charged with that crime when sentenced to death.

7 There is evidence suggesting that in America publicized executions actually inspire people to commit murder, thus brutalizing people in a particularly dramatic way. See Bowers, William J. and Pierce, Glenn L. (1980) 'Deterrence and Brutalization: What is the Effect of Executions?', *Crime and Delinquency*, 26, pp. 453–84. This evidence is inconclusive; see Phillips, David P. (1980) 'The Deterrent Effect of Capital Punishment: New Evidence on an Old Controversy', *The American Journal of Sociology*.

8 Reiman, J. (1986) 'Justice, Civilization and the Death Penalty', *Philosophy and Public Affairs*, 14, pp. 115–48.

9 *Ibid.*, p. 138.

10 *Ibid.*, p. 116.

11 I do not say the argument is attractive, only that it can be constructed. See Nozick, R. (1974) *Anarchy, State and Utopia*, Basil Blackwell.

12 Teddy Taylor chided some of his colleagues for inconsistently voting against the death penalty as too macabre a form of deterrence, and yet voting for the 'spending of billions of pounds on horrifying instruments of [nuclear war]' (p. 328, col. 627). It was unclear why Taylor thought the parallel had to count in favour of voting for the death penalty rather than against voting for spending on nuclear weapons.

CHAPTER THREE

Moral theory and moral theories

In the Parliamentary debate about the death penalty, points of moral principle tended to be assumed rather than argued for. Some speakers asserted that public distress would recede as the rate of violent crime declined, and they assumed that if it had the effect of reducing violent crime and relieving public distress, then capital punishment was justifiable. Supporters of the death penalty did not say why the relief of public distress mattered enough to cost anyone his life. But they were not alone in failing to give reasons. Gaps in justification were noticeable on the other side of the debate as well. Those who said that capital punishment was revenge and that revenge was always wrong did not meet the point that capital punishment might sometimes be deserved. Nor did they say why, if it *was* a case of getting even, it was wrong to get even with murderers or violent robbers. Can these gaps in justification be filled? Or is it a matter of take it or leave it when a point of moral principle is put forward in moral rhetoric? The answer is that justification sometimes can be given and that moral philosophy can be its source.

1 JUSTIFICATION AND MORAL THEORY

One of the purposes of moral philosophy is to give reasons for actions and judgements. This is reflected in normative ethical theories – structures of principles, rules and judgements concerning right and wrong – and in arguments bringing these structures to bear on particular cases. For example, a utilitarian normative ethics could have been invoked by many in the Parliamentary debate who argued for capital punishment as a deterrent to violent crime. Not that utilitarians must favour the death penalty, but their theory does lend itself to justifying the death penalty as a deterrent.

Utilitarianism identifies what it is right to do with whatever action in given circumstances has the best consequences. It understands by 'action with the best consequences' the one which produces the highest total benefit, the total being the sum of benefits to all of the individuals affected. Now individuals can be benefited by feeling less and less distress as the rate of violent crime decreases. What is more, this benefit to each individual, when summed up over all affected individuals, can outweigh the distress involved in reducing violent crime. Hence the utilitarian justification for capital punishment. If capital punishment deters violent criminals and the benefit to members of the general public exceeds the distress of the executed criminals and others affected by their deaths, then the execution of those criminals is right or at least morally permissible.

Opponents of the death penalty in the Parliamentary debate could have appealed to a moral theory of a different kind, for example one drawn from the New Testament. Arranged into precepts flowing from a principle about charity or love, Christ's ethical teaching is no harder to read as a normative ethical theory than utilitarianism. At least one speaker in the debate did invoke that teaching, although not in the form of an explicit theory. Ron Lewis said,

> I am not a virtuous person. I try to follow the dictates of my conscience and abide by the law, but there is one thing more important to me than the scriptures. I therefore pose this question. If the Lord Jesus, whom I profess to follow – I hope I do – with all my failings and faults, was in the House tonight, on whatever side, into which Lobby would he go? I have no hesitation in saying he would support the continued abolition of the death penalty. (p. 330, col. 631)

No doubt Lewis was right, given Christ's praise for charity

(I Corinthians, 13), forgiveness, and abstention from condemnation (Matthew, 7).

The availability of theories on both sides of the capital punishment debate raises a number of questions. How conclusively can a Christian principle justify the claim that capital punishment is wrong when a principle drawn from another theory, utilitarianism, say, justifies the contrary position? If any principle from any theory is going to have authority, do we not need to know the conditions under which one *theory* is to be preferred to another? And if so, are we not back where we started: might not the problem of deciding between different positions in moral rhetoric simply be reproduced at another level when we put the rhetorical claims in the context of appropriate and conflicting moral theories?

Theory, conflict of theories and acceptance

Though there are difficulties in deciding when a moral theory is acceptable or when one theory is to be preferred to another, it would be going too far to say that no theory ever gave a good reason for a moral claim, or that no theory ever established a moral claim as correct. Every standard moral theory says that murder is wrong and that lying is to be avoided. So from many different points of view, these claims are definitely correct. The theories may differ as regards what *makes* lying and murder wrong, but the fact that many different reasons can be given for not lying and for not murdering is compatible with their being many *good* reasons for saying it is wrong to lie or wrong to kill. Genuine problems arise when moral theories do not merely differ but conflict. When that happens we need a basis for deciding between theories, and it is not clear what that basis is to be.

In considering this problem it is important to get clear on the ground typically covered by a moral theory in philosophy. Adopting R. M. Hare's list of the topics that a theory is likeliest to discuss,[1] we may expect a theory to enlarge on a few or all of the following.

1 Philosophical methodology: i.e. what philosophy is supposed to be doing and how it does it.
2 Ethical analysis: i.e. the meanings of the moral words or the nature and logical properties of the moral concepts.
3 Moral methodology: i.e. how moral thinking ought to proceed, or how moral arguments and reasonings have to be conducted if they are to be cogent.
4 Normative moral questions: i.e. what we ought or ought not to do, what is just and unjust and so on.

When one moral theory says that capital punishment is right and another says that it is wrong, this is a conflict between answers to a quite specific 'normative moral question'. But such a conflict need not preclude the acceptance of a given moral theory, because theories are open to critical comparison under at least the three further headings (1) to (3). This means that indecision under heading number (4) is not necessarily indecision about which theory is preferable over all.

Even *within* the category of normative moral questions it may be possible to get acceptable general principles, principles about justice or rightness, for example. Or so it is sometimes claimed. According to John Rawls,[2] acceptable general principles are arrived at when they seem plausible in themselves, when no revision of them seems necessary in the light of particular moral judgements, and when particular moral judgements do not seem to require revision in the light of the principles. As long as no revision seems necessary, a state of what Rawls terms 'reflective equilibrium' is achieved, which permits the acceptance of the principles. A comparable sort of equilibrium, according to Rawls, attends the acceptance of hypotheses in the natural sciences. These are accepted for as long as they seem to be consistent with and to explain observations that there is no reason to distrust.

The analogy between moral principles and scientific hypotheses is not perfect, but this does not affect the point that the acceptance of moral principles can be well-grounded. The analogy falters because while observations are evidence for the truth of the hypotheses that explain them, particular moral judgements do not necessarily count toward the truth of principles that accord with and explain *them*. For example, at the time of writing it is possible to imagine that the considered moral judgements of many white people in South Africa are consistent with and are explained by the principles of apartheid. This fact, however, has no tendency to show that anyone's actions ought to be in keeping with the principles of apartheid. Whether particular moral judgements support principles depends on how the judgements are formed, what they are sensitive to. If they give undue weight to the interests of the people making the judgements, or if they are founded on factual error, then they have at best little authority, and none that rubs off on principles consistent with them. The principles must get their support not only from moral judgements, but from their meeting standards of objectivity and impartiality appropriate to the kinds of reasons for action they purport to be. Such standards exist. When principles meet the standards, acceptance of the principles is well-grounded.

The standards are represented in moral theories by various theoretical devices. Sometimes principles are required to be the sort that an impartial, benevolent observer might find acceptable. Other theories require that the principles be possible objects of choice for highly rational parties to a hypothetical social contract. Still others make it necessary that principles be the sort that one could want to have as laws of nature, activating everyone's behaviour in specified types of situation. As we will see shortly, some of these models are preferable to others. This means that there may be a better reason for accepting the principles of one theory than for accepting the principles of another.

Two further bases for theory choice may be mentioned. The first is to the effect that other things being equal, the simpler theory is the better. The second says that where two theories are otherwise similar, preference is to be given to the one whose coverage of moral experience is the more comprehensive.

Simplicity is sometimes thought to be desirable in any theory, but there are special reasons why it is thought to be a good thing in a moral theory. The reasons are to do with the drawbacks of Intuitionism, a theory according to which there can be many first principles of morality, all suggested by intuition. Since the appropriate *number* of first principles is also supposed to be suggested by intuition, there is no guarantee against having a large number. A large number may even be desirable from an Intuitionist point of view, since Intuitionists sometimes complain of the tendency of theories with a small number of principles to over-simplify. Yet, plainly, a theory that has no objection to having a principle for every situation stands to lose the generality required of a *theory*.

On the other hand, a standard background belief many people have about moral questions is that they are often not 'black and white' but ambiguous and complicated. No moral theory can be chosen for its simplicity if its simplicity results from ignoring the complication and the ambiguity of moral questions. What is worth choosing is a theory that avoids *unnecessary* complication: a theory can satisfy this condition and not be simple. Similarly, a theory that extends to more regions of moral experience than another but that treats none very sensitively, is not necessarily to be preferred to one that is narrower in scope but more accommodating of subtleties. So perhaps the right thing to demand is sensitivity in moral theory.

Supposing that requirements along the lines just sketched turn out to distinguish more from less acceptable moral theories, how might they apply in the conflict between, for example, utilitarianism and a theory organized round Christ's admonition to love one's neighbour? With regard to the Christian theory it could be asked whether the injunction to love one's neighbour has any authority for someone who does not already accept certain doctrines about Christ's nature. If the answer is that prior acceptance of the doctrines *is* necessary, then, in the conflict between Christian ethics and utilitarianism, utilitarianism might be preferred on the ground that it was the simpler theory. One does not have to hold elaborate religious views to believe, as utilitarians do, that the thing to do above all is maximize welfare or relieve distress. On the other hand, Christian ethics might outdo utilitarianism in both comprehensiveness and sensitivity.

It may be difficult to decide between two theories in the abstract. Besides considering how they stand to one another in respect of simplicity and comprehensiveness, in respect of plausibility of general principles and the model safeguarding impartiality in their choice of principles, one may want to take account of the answers they suggest to normative ethical questions, such as that of the rightness of capital punishment. If the answers that one theory suggests are extremely difficult to accept even when the reasons for the answers are well understood, then an otherwise attractive theory – perhaps one that is attractive for its comprehensiveness or simplicity – may have to be rejected. Later I shall argue that considered in the abstract both utilitarianism and the main alternative to it are objectionable. But further considerations, more specific to a concrete moral issue, namely the rightness of capital punishment, will tip the balance. They will underline the shortcomings of utilitarianism, and will start to reveal the strengths of a non-utilitarian theory. Eventually a non-utilitarian theory will be chosen as the more acceptable of the theories of capital punishment examined. But it will not be claimed to be the last word on capital punishment, let alone the best moral theory.

2 FROM THEORY TO THEORIES

The two accounts to be reviewed in detail – utilitarianism and Kantianism – conflict in important ways even though they can be used to justify superficially similar positions in the capital punishment debate; a first task will be to clarify the two theories, identify points of disagreement between them, and decide whether one has greater initial appeal than the other.

Utilitarianism

Utilitarianism assumes that various different outcomes of action can be located on a scale from best to worst, and it assumes that rankings according to this scale are objective. It goes on to identify right actions, the ones one ought morally to do, with those whose outcomes in the circumstances are best. Because utilitarianism makes rightness depend on the outcomes or consequences of actions, it is sometimes called a *consequentialist* theory. Because it makes the rightness of an action depend on a type of good at which the action aims, it is sometimes called a *teleological* theory (from the Greek word '*telos*', meaning end or thing aimed at). The good that right actions are supposed to aim at, according to utilitarianism, is the greatest total of benefits to individuals. According to how these benefits are conceived, different versions of utilitarianism can be distinguished. A benefit may be identified with a balance of pleasure over pain in an individual. On this interpretation, characteristic of the classical utilitarianism of Jeremy Bentham and John Stuart Mill, benefits to individuals must register in their conscious mental states, characteristically in feelings of pleasure and pain. It is possible, however, to conceive of a benefit as a satisfied or fulfilled desire, where satisfied desire need not involve conscious pleasure or indeed any other conscious states. Desire-utilitarianism usually allows the amount of benefit to vary with the strength of desire, so that the stronger the desire satisfied, the greater the benefit. It also tends to confine itself to desires an agent would have if he were properly informed. So in one version of utilitarianism an action is right if, out of all the available courses of action, it would produce the highest total pleasure. In the other version of utilitarianism the action that would produce the greatest amount of satisfaction of desire would be right and all other actions wrong.

Although there are many difficulties involved in formulating either version of utilitarianism, these are not usually thought to be insurmountable, and even the most unrelenting critics of utilitarianism are prepared to admit that its *prima facie* attractions are considerable. Bernard Williams has identified a number of such attractions, beginning with what he calls the 'non-transcendental character' of utilitarianism. The theory, Williams says, 'makes no appeal outside human life, in particular not to religious considerations. It thus helps, in particular, with the entirely reasonable demand that morality now should be obviously free of Christianity'.[3] Williams also mentions its promise of making all moral issues determinable in principle by the empirical calculation of consequences,[4] and its providing in pleasure, desire fulfilment or welfare, 'a common currency of moral thought'. In other words, Williams interprets utilitarianism as implying, plausibly enough, that whatever matters morally makes a difference to someone's or many people's happiness, welfare or desires or pleasure.

The attractions do not stop there. It is sometimes held that by making the consequences for the public welfare or total individual benefit the measure of right action, utilitarianism both expresses and tries to encourage in others an attitude of generalized benevolence.[5] This claim sits uneasily with an objection that is commonly made against utilitarianism, namely, that it permits the satisfaction of evil desires and positively demands it when the desires are felt by many people or felt intensely by a few. The thought that utilitarianism panders to the lynch mob or to the immoral majority is not borne out on reflection, for perhaps on utilitarian grounds *not* all desires have a claim to be satisfied. Desires for vengeance may be excluded as well as wishes to vent rage, for there may be some reason to think that vengeance and the venting of rage are usually outweighed by the satisfaction of other desires.

Even when there are restrictions on the desires that matter to its calculations, utilitarianism seems to permit actions that are not benevolent. In part this is because many different kinds of treatment of people are compatible with maximizing the general happiness or satisfaction of desires and some of these can involve the 'sacrifice' of individual happiness or satisfaction of desires. There is nothing in classical utilitarianism to prohibit the deliberate infliction of pain or suffering if it results in a net saving of pain or suffering. And, again from a classical utilitarian point of view, there is nothing *directly* wrong with killing, though its side-effects may show that in many or most cases it does not promote the general well-being.[6]

Now it is possible that desire-utilitarianism can exploit

the strength of the desire not to suffer pain in order to narrow the scope in classical utilitarianism for the rightful infliction of pain. It is possible, too, that desire-utilitarianism can exploit the strength of the desire not to die, and the fact that death commonly interferes with the satisfaction of many other desires, to narrow the scope in classical utilitarianism for permissible or rightful killing. But it is hard to see how even desire-utilitarianism can fail to recommend the infliction of pain when sufficiently many strong desires would be satisfied as a result, and it is hard to see how, in the same circumstances, it could prohibit killing, even the killing of an innocent person. The restriction of relevant desires to properly informed ones does not necessarily help in this connection.

To illustrate the point that in utilitarianism even the killing of the innocent is not beyond the pale, critics sometimes take the case of the atom bombs dropped on Japanese cities in World War Two. At the time and afterwards, the dropping of the bombs was justified on the ground that it shortened the war and therefore prevented more suffering and loss of life than it caused. Many who admitted that the cost in lives, including innocent lives, was very high, thought that the costs of a protracted war with Japan would have been even higher. Even if they were right the means adopted in shortening the war seem utterly brutal.

Cases like the one just mentioned are often taken to show that an acceptable moral theory must prohibit some courses of action whatever their consequences. Because utilitarianism imposes no absolutist prohibitions, it is sometimes thought to be an unacceptable moral theory. But it is not obvious that the absolutist position is correct, or that it succeeds in identifying what is really objectionable in utilitarianism. In considering whether absolutism is correct, it is worth asking whether its prohibitions are reasonable when the consequences of complying with them are unthinkably awful. For example, would the killing of the innocent be beyond the pale even in the case where not to do so would bring about a nuclear holocaust? Again, it can be asked whether absolutism accurately diagnoses what is wrong with utilitarianism. Perhaps the problem is not, as absolutism suggests, that the rightness and wrongness of actions is left to be decided by the consequences. Perhaps what is wrong is that it requires the performance of a hideous action even when its benefits are only marginally greater than those of a much more palatable alternative action.

Whichever objection is closer to the mark, utilitarians need to answer the charge that they too often let the public welfare justify the unpalatable action. The objection is likely to be pressed strongly not only in connection with a utilitarian defence of the death penalty, but also a utilitarian defence of punishment in general. Since to inflict punishment is necessarily to do something painful or undesirable to the person being punished, how can it ever be justified by a theory that prides itself on expressing benevolence? In classical utilitarianism the tension is supposed to be resolved by appealing to deterrence or, more generally, the preventive effect of punishment. Jeremy Bentham sketches the relevant line of thought in his *Principles of Penal Law*:

> General prevention ought to be the chief end of punishment as it is its real justification. If we could consider an offence which has been committed as an isolated fact, the like of which would never recur, punishment would be useless. It would only be adding one evil to another. But when we consider that an unpunished crime leaves the path of crime open, not only to the same delinquent but also to all those who may have the same motives and opportunities for entering upon it, we perceive that punishment inflicted on the individual becomes the source of security to all. That punishment which considered in itself appeared base and repugnant to all generous sentiments is elevated to the first rank of benefits when it is regarded not as an act of wrath or vengeance against a guilty or unfortunate individual who has given way to mischievous inclinations, but as an indispensable sacrifice to the common safety.[7]

Whether even extremely severe punishment, like hanging, is supposed to be an 'indispensable sacrifice' is not clear from the passage. This is because it is unclear from the passage whether *any* punishment is an 'indispensable sacrifice'. The common safety is a good, certainly, but it needs to be shown that it is so great a good that even an extremely painful punishment is justified by it.

I have been labouring a certain problem about ends and means. A further difficulty for utilitarianism concerns the way in which it adds together the benefits and costs of various courses of action to determine which is the best available. In a utilitarian calculation the fact that benefits and costs are benefits and costs for different people falls out of consideration. One simply chooses the action that has the highest total benefit, regardless of whether the costs of so acting fall disproportionately on one person. To illustrate this, consider a case in which a patient can only have his life prolonged by a treatment that is extremely expensive. So expensive is it that for the same cost eighty people can have their lives made considerably more pleasant. Where the difference made to the eighty is considerable and there is only the sum of money for doing one thing or the other, we can imagine utilitarianism directing us to spend it on the eighty rather than on the one. The fact that the *life* of the one is in the balance is obscured in the utilitarian calculation, for the calculation takes account only of the total cost or benefit, not whether it is so unevenly distributed as to create injustice. Yet it is very plausible to hold that there are limits to acceptable trade-offs between costs and benefits, and that this limit is reached when a person's life is sacrificed, or short of this, when his well-being declines below an acceptable minimum. This limit on trade-offs is unlikely to be met in utilitarianism because it does not naturally have minimum well-being per person as a frame of reference. In that sense it does not recognize the separateness of persons; it lumps together the well-being of different persons.[8]

Consequentialist and deontological theories

Deontological theories get round some of the difficulties that face consequentialist theories such as utilitarianism. To begin with their defining characteristic, deontological theories hold that certain actions are right or wrong quite apart from the good consequences they would produce or the bad consequences they would prevent. A deontological theory is thus the natural framework for justifying the claim that the bombing of Hiroshima was wrong, wrong even if it did shorten World War Two. In the same way, deontological theories do not have to strain to say what makes the killing of the innocent wrong: they all specify certain forms of treatment of human beings, including the killing of the innocent, as wrong in themselves.

Certain deontological theories may also be better equipped than consequentialism to say what is wrong with killing. The reason is that these theories throw light on the worth of a life and thus on what is lost when a life is taken away. In the thinking behind the doctrine of the virtues in Christian ethics,[9] for example, each person's life affords the possibility of salvation from sin and the possibility of seeking to know and love God. These possibilities make each life valuable and help to explain why the deliberate curtailment of a life is evil. Not all deontological theories, however, carry with them as elaborate a theory of the worth of a life as the one implicit in the Christian ethics. According to early rights theories associated with liberal individualism it seems to have been taken as a brute fact that one's life was valuable.[10]

While only some deontological theories are able to give a substantive account of the worth of life, all seem to acknowledge the separateness of persons in a way consequentialism cannot. In Christian ethics, for example,

> a man is not merely a representative object who has significance because he shares a common, undifferentiated ingredient, namely human nature. He is a highly individualized creation, uniquely particular: and no matter how much the group needs to be respected and taken into account, yet the particularity of the person must never be completely lost sight of.[11]

One reason why the individual is particularly important, according to Christian teaching, is that the creation of each human life depends in some sense on divine intervention. Another reason is that chances of redemption come through individual lives.

Kant

Other deontological theories recognize the separateness of persons without expressing its significance in theological terms. Thus Kant's moral philosophy contains the concept of a 'realm of ends', a 'systematic union of different rational beings through common laws'.[12] The inhabitants of Kant's realm of ends are called 'persons' in the special sense that their nature indicates that they are not to be used for the arbitrary purposes of other individuals. In the realm of ends each person is supposed to be an object of respect for every other. Among other things this means that there is no end for which a person can be sacrificed, there being no end that is more valuable than a sacrificed person.[13] The realm of ends is a model of relations between morally upright individuals, and so it functions as an ideal for individuals who are not completely upright but who have a rational nature worthy of respect in common with those who are. The realm of ends is not merely an association of rational beings but a union of them through common laws.[14] Each person is supposed to be both a maker and an obeyer of certain common laws of conduct. And because to comply with laws is to comply with laws they each make, people in the realm of ends are free or autonomous: they enjoy self-rule. At the same time, however, they are constrained: the laws that any one person frames must be compatible with a higher law calling upon each to 'treat himself and all others never merely as a means but in every case also as an end in himself'.[15]

The requirement never to treat another merely as a means is hard to satisfy in practice. Surely when I take a bus or order a meal in a restaurant I treat the driver or the waiter as a means: what it would be also to treat them as ends in themselves is unclear. Indeed, even apart from cases where the contacts between people are too slight or too distorted by the roles being played for Kant's requirement to be met straightforwardly, it is none too clear what it is to treat someone as an end in himself. Perhaps it consists in doing to another only those actions that he could will to be done to himself. Kant appears to be driving at this in *The*

Foundations of the Metaphysics of Morals where he explains what is wrong with making deceitful promises to another or attacking his freedom or property. The person at the receiving end of the deceit or attack, he suggests, could never make the aim of such treatment his own. In Kant's words, 'he whom I want to use for my purposes . . . cannot possibly assent to my mode of acting against him and cannot contain the end of this action in himself'.[16] Where it is oneself one mistreats, Kant does not postulate a true or real underlying self who could not possibly assent to what one does; instead, he invokes the humanity present in oneself and speaks of offences against it.[17] Humanity and not just the individual human being is an end in itself. Kant thought it was only necessary for people to contemplate themselves in order to get the idea of a being who could not be used or suited to other people's purposes.[18] From the conception of an end in itself it was supposed to be possible to derive specific laws of the will capable of yielding moral conduct.

Kant's talk of humans or rational beings as ends in themselves can be roughly summarized as follows: the fact that certain individuals are human or rational is by itself sufficient reason for doing what morality requires. He wanted to deny that human beings had to have some further incentive, something over and above the recognition of humanity or reason, in order to do what morality required. In particular, he wanted to deny that a feeling of love for humanity or a capacity for sympathizing with other human beings, was a part of genuinely moral motivation.

The claim that people are entitled to certain forms of treatment just on account of their humanity is open to a number of interpretations. It could mean that, being members of the biological species *homo sapiens*, people are liable to be damaged by certain forms of treatment and helped by others, and that the damage of the one sort of treatment and the benefit of the other is a sufficient reason for omitting the one and extending the other. Again, it may be that as members of the biological species people have certain needs – for food, shelter, etc. – and that the badness of not having these needs fulfilled is a reason for giving people the help that *would* fulfil them. This biological basis for deserving good treatment is not what Kant has in mind. The treatment that people are meant to receive in the realm of ends is due not to their biological nature but to a supposedly quite distinct rational nature. More specifically, the quality of the practical reason of people in the realm of ends – the way they use reason to make practical choices – is supposed to determine how they are treated. People have a claim to benevolent treatment in the realm of ends because each acts according to policies that could coherently be willed to be acted upon always by everyone in similar circumstances. In other words, their claim to be treated well depends on their behaving according to policies that are universalizable and that reason can therefore establish as unconditionally acceptable.

Each member of the realm of ends both frames and is subject to universalizable laws of conduct, and this constitutes relations of mutual respect between agents. Each willingly confines the policies of action he adopts to ones that do not use other agents as means. And the reason each observes this restriction is that each recognizes the worth of the self-rule of other members of the realm of ends. Each recognizes the next person's status as a free or autonomous agent. As Kant puts it, summarizing the entire line of thought about the realm of ends, 'Autonomy is the basis of the dignity of both human nature and every rational nature'.[19]

The autonomous or self-ruling will that Kant makes so much of is a very pure will, in two senses of 'pure'. First, its determination to do what morality demands (what is universalizable) and to omit what morality prohibits is unshakeable. It is as morally pure as a non-holy will can be. Second, in trying to do what is right the will is supposed to be unaffected by any empirical inducement. It is supposed to be bent on doing the moral thing independently of natural impulses that assist right action (such as sympathy or benevolence) and in spite of natural impulses that get in the way of right action (such as self-love). So it is pure in the second and unusual sense of being untainted by anything empirical or natural. Kant believed that this supernatural rational will, this capacity for firm self-rule, belonged to any being capable of moral agency, that is, any being capable of action for the sake of duty alone. Moreover, he thought that the operation of this rational will was actually visible in many simple, pious people, and that it was present, though not conspicuous, in others who were not ideally motivated to do right. Among those who were not ideally motivated to do right he included not only the cold-hearted and unfriendly, but also, and perhaps surprisingly, the naturally outgoing and sympathetic. He believed that people of this last sort were under a pathological necessity to do a certain kind of action, not motivated by moral requirements. When they did something demanded by morality they did it not because morality demanded it but because they were naturally constituted to be kind and loving. Their good nature acted through them, so to speak, whether they liked it or not. Real moral worth was to be found in those whose good actions owed nothing to a fortunate constitution. It was to be found, for example, in the cold and unsympathetic person who by a gargantuan effort did the right thing against all of his inclinations, or in the absence of any inclinations, just because he saw it was his duty to do so.

Kant held that impulses encouraging good actions were neither widely enough distributed nor reliable enough in those who enjoyed them to enable all of those who were obliged to do the right thing to do it. There had to be something other than inclinations enabling one to behave morally and this was the capacity for acting according to the determination of reason: If the ability to behave morally depended on a capacity that human beings could naturally lack, or on a capacity that some could naturally exercise more readily than others, then the fortunate possession of the capacity would make morality easier for some than for others. Natural advantage would translate into moral advantage, contrary to the idea that it is equally within the power of every rational agent to act rightly.[20]

The line of thought that leads Kant to postulate a non-empirical will as the thing subject to moral demands is very profound and to some extent persuasive; but if a theory were able to acknowledge the separateness of persons and keep natural advantage from turning into moral advantage *without* so obscure and metaphysical an understanding of the autonomous will, that theory would probably be preferable to Kant's. Rawls has claimed that his theory of justice as fairness is highly Kantian,[21] and that its device of an 'original position' is an attempt to interpret Kant's conception of a rationally chosen moral law.[22]

Rawls's 'Kantian Theory'

Rawls is concerned to give principles for evaluating social institutions as just or unjust. He thinks that a given set of institutions will meet the demands of justice if free, equal and rational agents could originally have chosen those institutions in fair circumstances. Circumstances of choice are supposed to be fair if parties to the choice are mutually disinterested and if they are deprived of certain morally irrelevant information about themselves and the standing they will have in a society embodying the institutions chosen. In the so-called 'original position', the position in which the choice of institutions is made, a 'veil of ignorance' is supposed to conceal from the parties to the choice facts about their individual talents, income, race, sex, forebears, even their particular views of the good things in life. The idea behind keeping these things dark is that of fairness: it would be unfair if a given choice of social institutions were informed by knowledge of social and natural contingencies that could lead certain of the choosers to give themselves special advantages.

While the knowledge of the parties in the original position is very restricted – the parties are even ignorant of the degree of development of the society whose institutions they are choosing – Rawls's theory grants them some general knowledge of economics, politics and sociology, and also knowledge of some goods – the primary ones – that will advance the life-plans of individuals regardless of their particular conceptions of the good life. With this mix of knowledge and ignorance individuals in the original position are supposed to be able to choose two principles to judge the justice of institutions by. The first principle calls for institutions to allow the greatest equal liberty compatible with a like liberty for all. The second principle permits economic and social advantages to be distributed unevenly only where it benefits everyone and specifically those with least.

The consequences of these principles are worked out by Rawls in considerable detail, but they do not need to be considered for his claim about the Kantian character of his theory to be understood. Here in part is Rawls's account of the relation between his own views and Kant's:

> Kant held, I believe, that a person is acting autonomously when the principles of his action are chosen by him as the most adequate possible expression of his nature as a free and equal rational being. The principles he acts upon are not adopted because of his social position or natural endowments, or in view of the particular kind of society in which he lives or the specific things that he happens to want ... Assuming, then, that the reasoning in favor of the principles of justice is correct, we can say that when people act on these principles they are acting in accordance with principles that they would choose as rational and independent persons in an original position of equality. The principles of their actions do not depend upon social or natural contingencies, nor do they reflect the bias of the particulars of their plan of life or the aspirations that motivate them. By acting from these principles persons express their nature as free and equal rational beings subject to the general conditions of human life. For to express one's nature as a being of a particular kind is to act on the principles that would be chosen if this nature were the decisive determining element. Of course, the choice of the parties in the original position is subject to the restrictions of that situation. But when we knowingly act on the principles of justice in the ordinary course of events, we deliberately assume the limitations of the original position. One reason for doing this, for persons who can do so and want to, is to express their nature as free and equal rational beings.[23]

It is unclear whether the idea of expressing one's nature is to be found in Kant's idea of autonomy. Rawls seems to *reinterpret* the Kantian conception of acting autonomously. For Rawls, to act autonomously is not, as in Kant, to have one's actions prompted by the rational rather than the passionate part of one's nature. It is to have one's actions prompted by a view of the good unbiased by information about one's own specific tastes, aptitudes and situation.

Rawls is not committed, as Kant is, to a will or reason devoid of all empirical characteristics, but the nature that is supposed to be expressed in Rawlsian autonomous activity is still quite stripped down, because all that is assumed to be true of Rawlsian agents is that they are free, equal and able to make rational choices. Rawls does not make the utilitarian mistake of agglomerating or conflating these figures, but he does seem to be guilty of preserving a separateness of excessively abstract or schematic persons. This is because he makes too much information about different agents morally irrelevant according to his theory. In particular the rational choice of institutions is supposed to be unaffected by information about individual conceptions of the good, or conceptions of the good more detailed than one geared to the primary goods. There are sound reasons for thinking, however, that a very thin conception of the good, such as is confined to the primary goods, favours some life-plans unfairly.[24] Rawls must either allow more information concerning conceptions of the good to come out from under the veil of ignorance, thus compromising the fairness of the choice situation, or he must preserve a separateness of excessively abstract persons. A related but less high flown objection, this time invited by Rawls and Kant equally, is that by populating their theoretical situations with very abstract or under-specified persons they preserve the separateness, while leaving out the individuality, of persons.[25]

As in Kant's theory, so in Rawls's, agents are supposed to stand to one another in relations of mutual respect.[26] In particular, agents are supposed to respect one another's autonomy. But it is not clear why respect should be the preferred type of moral relation between persons or the mainspring of justice. Concern for another's welfare rather than respect might be preferable in theory as the basic moral attitude,[27] first because it extends to a wider array of creatures than those that can inspire respect;[28] second, because it is less artificial, not being constrained to be insensitive to all but the non-contingent aspects of the beings to whom it is directed.

Further problems attend perhaps the most distinctive feature of a Kantian moral theory: its use of universalizability as a test of whether a given policy of action is right or not. When we wonder whether a type of action is one that we ought, morally ought, to undertake, Kant's theory invites us to ask two questions about it. Is the policy of action one that could be made into a self-consistent law binding on everyone whose circumstances were of the same kind as mine? In other words, would it be self-consistent to suppose that everyone in my circumstances could be determined to act as I propose to? If the answer is 'Yes', I *might* have a morally correct policy. Whether I have one in fact depends on the answer to a second question. Could I coherently *want* everyone in circumstances like my own to be bound by my policy of action? For example, could I coherently want to have universalized a policy of helping only oneself? There might be no actual contradiction in describing a state of affairs in which people helped only themselves, but since, on Kant's assumptions, people are not self-sufficient, situations are bound to arise in which they want each other's help. No one, then, can coherently want the policy of self-help to be made universal. And since Kant thinks that it must be at least possible to want a morally correct policy of action to hold universally, the policy of self-help turns out not to be morally correct.[29] The 'want' test of universalizability helps to save Kant from the objection that he offers a purely formal test of the rightness of policies of action, but there is still room for the objection that universalizability tests can only get at some features of moral requirements.

Kant's tests are supposed to distinguish non-moral from moral requirements, where the latter are considered to be 'categorical imperatives' – precepts obliging us *unconditionally* to do or omit certain things. Kant denies the status of moral requirements to hypothetical imperatives, that is, precepts that require us to do things *if* we have certain desires. But at least one philosopher, Phillipa Foot, has challenged the picture of moral obligation that underlies this distinction between hypothetical and categorical imperatives. Kant

wanted to capture the inescapability of moral requirements by making their bindingness independent of desire: Foot has wondered whether this kind of inescapability is clearly conceivable.[30]

3 TAKING STOCK

It is clear that there are strains in the framework appropriate to the realm of ends and the original position. There are strains, too, in the relevant conception of persons or moral agents. There are possible objections to Kant's test of universalizability as well as to his idea of the categorical imperative. A Kantian theory is not the only possible form a deontological normative ethics can take – Christian normative ethics is deontological – and so difficulties in formulating a deontological theory do not necessarily force a retreat to utilitarianism. But Kantian theories are usually regarded as the leading alternatives to utilitarian ones. This chapter has suggested that they are not overwhelmingly superior to utilitarian theories when both utilitarian and Kantian theories are considered in the abstract. In the remainder of this book we shall see whether one sort of theory proves more acceptable than the other when both are applied to a concrete problem – that of the morality of capital punishment.

NOTES

1 Hare, R. M., 'Rawls' Theory of Justice', in Daniels, N. (ed.) (1975) *Reading Rawls*, Basil Blackwell, p. 81.
2 Rawls, *op. cit.*, p. 69.
3 Williams, Bernard (1972) *Morality: An Introduction to Ethics*, Cambridge University Press, p. 97.
4 *Ibid.*, pp. 98–9.
5 Smart, in Smart, J. J. C. and Williams, Bernard (1973) *Utilitarianism: For and Against*, Cambridge University Press, p. 7.
6 On the failure of utilitarianism to come to grips adequately with the wrongness of killing, see Frey, R. G. (1984) *Utility*

and Rights, Basil Blackwell, pp. 13–19 and Griffin, J. (1982) 'Bentham and Modern Utilitarianism', *Revue Internationale de Philosophie*, 36, pp. 366–7.

7 Bowring, J. (ed.) *The Works of Jeremy Bentham*, vol. I, p. 383, quoted in Honderich, Ted (1976, 2nd edn) *Punishment: The Supposed Justifications*, Penguin, pp. 51–2.

8 Rawls, *op. cit.*, p. 27 and p. 29.

9 I have relied on Geach, P. (1977) *The Virtues*, Cambridge University Press.

10 For an account of early liberal rights theories, see MacIntyre, Alasdair (1967) *A Short History of Ethics*, Routledge & Kegan Paul, chapters 11 and 12.

11 Carpenter, Canon E. F., 'The Christian Context', in Blom-Cooper, Louis (ed.) (1969) *The Hanging Question*, Duckworth, p. 35.

12 Kant, Immanuel (1785) *The Foundations of the Metaphysics of Morals*, L. J. Beck (trans.) Bobbs-Merrill, 1969 edn, p. 433. Page references are to the Akademie edition.

13 *Ibid.*, p. 428.

14 *Ibid.*, p. 433.

15 *Ibid.*

16 *Ibid.*, pp. 429–30.

17 *Ibid.*, p. 429.

18 *Ibid.*

19 *Ibid.*, p. 437.

20 For a discussion in more detail of the matters raised in this paragraph, see Sorell, Tom (1987) 'Kant's Good Will and Our Good Nature', *Kant-Studien*, 78.

21 Rawls, *op. cit.*, p. viii.

22 *Ibid.*, p. 252.

23 *Ibid.*, pp. 252–3.

24 See Nagel, Thomas, 'Rawls on Justice', reprinted in Daniels, *op. cit.*, pp. 8–10.

25 See Williams, Bernard, 'Persons, Character and Morality', reprinted in Williams, Bernard (1981) *Moral Luck*, Cambridge University Press, pp. 4–5.

26 Rawls, *op. cit.*, p. 179 and p. 256.

27 For the distinction between concern and respect, see Harris, *op. cit.*, p. 2.

28 In particular to non-human animals, who are felt in advance of theory to have moral claims on us.

29 For a defence of this interpretation of Kant and much else on the two tests, see Paul Dietrichson's excellent article, 'Kant's

Criteria of Universalizability', reprinted in Wolff, R. P. (ed.) (1969) *Kant: Foundations of the Metaphysics of Morals: Text and Critical Essays*, Bobbs-Merrill, pp. 163–207.

30 See her 'Morality as a System of Hypothetical Imperatives', reprinted in Foot, P. (1978) *Virtues and Vices*, Basil Blackwell, pp. 157–73.

CHAPTER FOUR

Utilitarianism and the death penalty

Utilitarians identify morally right actions with those that in the circumstances bring about the greatest benefits. Thus, when an agent is faced with alternative courses of action each of which is beneficial, and one is, perhaps only marginally, more beneficial than the other, utilitarianism holds that the more beneficial is morally right to perform and the other morally wrong to perform. This is so even where, intuitively, the action with the slightly more beneficial results is the more unsavoury of the two. Thus, if lying to a patient would spare him one hour's anxiety, telling the truth at the last moment would spare him only forty minutes of anxiety, and there is otherwise nothing to distinguish the consequences of the two courses of action, utilitarianism calls for the lie. Similarly, if by quietly ignoring the terms of a will one would add two fine pictures to an already excellent public collection, while only one would be added if the terms were respected, utilitarianism can recommend that the terms of the will be quietly ignored. Finally, and to come to the justification used by utilitarian defenders of the death penalty, if the execution of murderers deters more people from murdering than any lesser punishment, then execution, though an evil, is a necessary evil. It is necessary even if a lesser punishment deters a significant number of criminals.

The utilitarian position has considerable appeal, for it grants something to those who think that life is sacred and something also to those who think that murderers should die. To those who think that life is sacred it concedes that capital punishment is an evil and that very good reasons are needed for visiting it on anyone; to those who think that murderers ought to die it concedes that good, indeed decisive, reasons for executing killers *can* be given: reasons demonstrating a bigger deterrent effect than imprisonment and therefore the possibility of a net saving of life.

Despite its initial attractions this position is not acceptable to all utilitarians, let alone all supporters of execution. This is because it leans heavily on the assumption that capital punishment is an effective preventive measure. To utilitarians who find this assumption implausible, the death penalty must appear not as a necessary evil, but an evil pure and simple. The position can also seem unacceptable to *non*-utilitarians who support the death penalty. The reason is that the utilitarian justification for capital punishment ignores the culpability of murderers and violent criminals and the harm already done to the victim and those who care about the victim. Instead of looking at the blood that has already been spilt, utilitarianism looks to the future to see what can be done to prevent other people suffering as the previous victims have. In this chapter, I shall consider some utilitarian arguments for the death penalty from J. S. Mill, and some recent utilitarian arguments against the death penalty from Jonathan Glover. I shall claim that Mill's position is the stronger of the two but also that it is not thoroughly utilitarian. Then I shall argue that it is the stronger position *because* it departs from utilitarianism. This will prepare the ground for a discussion of non-utilitarian arguments for and against the death penalty in later chapters.

1 MILL'S SPEECH

John Stuart Mill gave a powerful speech in favour of the retention of capital punishment in a British parliamentary debate of 1868.[1] Although some of his arguments make use of the familiar idea of deterring would-be criminals, they are not merely early versions of deterrence arguments put forward in the 1980s. Mill's use of the idea of deterrence is out of the ordinary, out of the ordinary without being out of date. His views are not based solely on deterrence. At one point he wonders whether his fellow Parliamentarians are not too shocked by death; elsewhere he asks whether not continuing to exist matters more than living in suffering. These sidelines in his speech lend it a depth and breadth noticeably absent from contributions to the 1982 debate.

Mill's main argument is that for the particularly serious crime of murder, execution can sometimes be both the most appropriate and the most humane punishment. The 'sometimes' is important. He does not claim that all convicted murderers should be put to death, only those found guilty of what he calls 'aggravated murder' – particularly brutal murder carried out in cold blood.

> When there has been brought home to any one, by conclusive evidence, the greatest crime known to the law; and when the attendant circumstances suggest no palliation of the guilt, no hope that the culprit may even yet not be unworthy to live among mankind, nothing to make it probable that the crime was a general exception to his general character rather than a consequence of it, then I confess it appears to me that to deprive the criminal of the life of which he has proved to be unworthy – solemnly to blot him out from the fellowship of mankind – is the most appropriate, as it is certainly the most impressive, mode in which the society can attach to so great a crime the penal consequences which for the security of life it is indispensable to annex to it.[2]

Mill made these remarks about seven years after he had published *Utilitarianism*, but is the point of view expressed a utilitarian one? There is room for uncertainty, because of the factors that are supposed to make the taking of a murderer's life 'appropriate'. On the one hand Mill talks about depriving the criminal of the life of which he has 'proved unworthy'. On the other hand he mentions the penal consequences that have to be attached to aggravated murder for the sake of the security of a society. The argument from security is recognizably a utilitarian one, for security is naturally a component of the public welfare and in utilitarianism what contributes most to the public welfare or the total amount of happiness or desire-satisfaction is what is morally right. The problem with the argument from security is that it is not obviously an argument for capital punishment. Why would not life imprisonment for the brutal murderer protect society just as effectively as execution? Here, presumably, is where the argument from appropriateness comes in. Mill may be relying, between the lines, on the following piece of reasoning: 'Aggravated murder is specially awful; so its punishment should be severer than punishment for less heinous kinds of murder. Life imprisonment fits less heinous kinds of murder; so it cannot be appropriate to aggravated murder; the death penalty, rightly reserved for the worst crime, fits aggravated murder, for that is the worst crime.'

About the argument from appropriateness two questions arise. One concerns its consistency with utilitarianism; the other has to do with the harshness of the penalty that is said to be appropriate: is the inhumanity of brutal murder not compounded by the judicial killing of brutal murderers? In his speech Mill took up the second question but not the first. The first question arises because the argument from appropriateness seems to be retributivist, and retributivist positions differ from utilitarian ones both in temporal perspective and in the ground of right and wrong they assume.

Retributivist positions look backward in time. They assume that the past suffering of victims of crime can be cancelled out or counter-balanced by things done in the present. And they go further to hold that it is good for past suffering to be cancelled out or counter-balanced, even if no one now is affected by the past suffering, even if it is all water under the bridge. The retributivist departure from the utilitarian framework is clearest where victim and wrongdoer both suffer losses, the wrongdoer suffers losses because the victim does, but the wrongdoer's loss is not the victim's gain or anyone else's gain either. This seems to be the position where the wrongdoer is executed for murder, no one cares enough about the murder victim to want the killing avenged, and no difference will be made to the subsequent murder rate by the publicity of the execution.

Think of the murder of some old man living rough without friends or relatives. Retributivists hold that in such a case a debt is still owed and must be paid even if doing so satisfies no desires and contributes in no clear way to the public welfare. The reality of the debt and the need to discharge it are independent of whether people happen to care: what makes the debt real and creates the obligation to pay is the harm done to the victim – independently of anything else. By contrast, utilitarianism denies that the bindingness of a moral obligation is *ever* independent of whether anyone cares. In the sort of case under discussion utilitarianism may even deny that there is any direct reason for punishing the murderer. It may clutch at the bad side-effects of allowing a murderer to get away with it; but if no real difference is made to the total of felt pleasure or the satisfaction of desire, there is, in utilitarian terms, little to justify taking action.

Mill's argument from appropriateness does sound retributivist and retributivism is non-utilitarian. Yet presumably Mill wanted to argue for the death penalty on utilitarian grounds. The problem is not serious if a good case for the death penalty remains when retributivist-sounding arguments are subtracted from Mill's speech. And at first sight a case for the death penalty does remain. Mill argues that the death penalty is the best deterrent to aggravated murder and also that, despite appearances, it is less harsh and so more humane than life imprisonment with hard labour.

Deterrence

In his speech of 1868 Mill did not argue directly for the deterrent effect of the death penalty; instead, he tried to refute claims that it had no deterrent effect, claims made by fellow Parliamentarians and by others outside Parliament. Here is his first argument.

> My hon. Friend says that [capital punishment] does not inspire terror, and that experience proves it to be a failure. But the influence of a punishment is not to be measured by its effect on hardened criminals. Those whose habitual way of life keeps them, so to speak, at all times within the sight of the gallows, do grow to care less about it; as, to compare

> good things with bad, an old soldier is not much affected by the chance of dying in battle. I can afford to admit all that is often said about the indifference of professional criminals to the gallows. . . But the efficacy of a punishment which acts principally through the imagination, is chiefly to be measured by the impression it makes on those who are still innocent; by the horror with which it surrounds the first promptings of guilt; the restraining influence it exerts over the graded declension toward the state – never suddenly attained – in which crime no longer revolts, and punishment no longer terrifies.[3]

Eloquently stated though it is, the argument does not establish that the innocent are *put off* by the death penalty: the most it shows is that the reaction of the innocent to the death penalty – whatever that reaction is – is far more important to the case for capital punishment than the reaction of the hardened criminal. Mill insinuates, of course, that the innocent will shrink from doing anything punishable by death, since for them the thought of the gallows still has the power to terrify. But there is no necessary connection between being innocent and being horrified by the death penalty. Innocence in the relevant sense could consist of no more than never having set out to commit a crime. Now such innocence could exist in social conditions in which moderate violence was commonplace enough and extreme violence was portrayed often enough for execution to terrify no one. The objection does not only have force against the background of the newspapers, television and cinema of the 1980s. Mill opened his speech by saying that within his memory, 'rows of human beings might be seen suspended in front of Newgate by those who ascended or descended Ludgate Hill'.[4] Presumably passers-by such as Mill could have become hardened to the spectacle without conceiving criminal intentions.

Mill's second argument against those who doubted the deterrent effect of capital punishment had to do with the inconspicuousness of the deterrent effect.

> As for what is called the failure of the death punishment, who is able to judge of that? We partly know who those are whom it has not deterred; but who is there who knows

> whom it has deterred, or how many human beings it has saved who would have lived to be murderers if that awful association had not been thrown round the idea of murder from their earliest infancy.[5]

This does no more than raise the possibility that many have been invisibly saved from becoming murderers by the horror of hanging. It does not show that anyone ever has been deterred and it asserts rather than establishes that where execution exists as the penalty, murder has awful associations.

Mill's final argument began with a concession. Capital punishment had indeed failed to deter when it had been applied to cases of theft, for

> the thief did not believe that it would be inflicted. He had learnt by experience that jurors would perjure themselves rather than find him guilty; that judges would seize any excuse for not sentencing him to death, or for recommending him to mercy; and that if neither jurors nor judges were merciful, there were still hopes from an authority above both. When things had come to this pass it was high time to give up the vain attempt. When it is impossible to inflict a punishment, or when its infliction becomes a public scandal, the idle threat cannot too soon disappear from the statute book.[6]

The threat of capital punishment for theft in England and Wales in the 1880s had failed to deter because it was an idle threat. Capital punishment for murder would also fail to deter, Mill added, if it, too, proved an idle threat. But judges and juries were not yet unwilling to inflict it, and so its deterrent effect was not to be minimized. Like the arguments already outlined this one is not very substantial. It may show that there is no extrapolating from the effect of the death penalty for one sort of crime to the effect of the death penalty for another sort of crime, but it does not establish what deterrent effect the death penalty has, or even that it has any.

Apparent and real harshness

Mill did not rest his case for capital punishment on deterrence arguments alone. He gave reasons for thinking that execution was a more humane punishment for aggravated murder than another that might have been thought suitable for purposes of deterrence, namely, imprisonment with hard labour for life. This is the most unusual and interesting of the arguments in Mill's speech, and it is worth examining in some detail.

The argument is given in support of the claim that hanging is the best penalty for aggravated murder.

> I defend this penalty, when confined to atrocious cases, on the very ground on which it is commonly attacked – on that of humanity to the criminal; as being beyond comparison the least cruel mode in which it is possible adequately to deter from the crime. If, in our horror of inflicting death, we endeavour to devise some punishment for the living criminal which shall act with a deterrent force at all comparable to that of death, we are driven to inflictions less severe indeed in appearance; and therefore less efficacious, but far more cruel in reality. Few, I think, would venture to propose, as a punishment for aggravated murder, less than imprisonment with hard labour for life; that is the fate to which a murderer would be consigned by the mercy which shrinks from putting him to death. But has it been sufficiently considered what sort of mercy this is, and what kind of life this leaves to him?[7]

Mill proceeds to argue that the apparently less severe penalty is in fact nothing of the kind. The 'short pang of a rapid death' is really not nearly so bad as hard labour for life, which involves

> immuring [the convicted murderer] in a living tomb, there to live out what may be a long life in the hardest and most monotonous toil, without any of its alleviations or rewards – debarred from all pleasant sights and sounds, and cut off from all earthly hope, except a slight mitigation of bodily restraint, or a small improvement of diet[.][8]

Against this background Mill claims that hard labour for life is really a more severe punishment than it seems, while the death penalty seems more severe than it is. He then invokes the interesting principle that

> it is the strongest recommendation a punishment can have that it should seem more rigorous than it is; for its practical power depends far less on what it is than on what it seems.[9]

From this it is only a short step to the conclusion that for both its power of deterrence and its actual mildness the death penalty is preferable to hard labour for life.

Mill's argument for the relative mildness of the death penalty is perhaps a little facile, and I shall mention some objections to it in a moment. I want to consider first his principle about the seeming severity of punishment. According to the principle a given punishment is to be preferred when it appears to be more rigorous than it is. Even if we accept this and grant Mill his further claim that capital punishment looks harsher than it actually is, it does not follow that capital punishment has very much to recommend it. On the contrary, to whatever degree the principle recommends execution, it recommends even more strongly a faked but convincing-looking execution, or the empty but convincing threat of execution. Or at least it does so as long as the apparently executed person or the person apparently condemned to death is punished somehow. For a faked but convincing-looking execution certainly appears to be more severe than it is, and since it will seem to the unsuspecting to be a real execution, it cannot be faulted for having less of a deterrent effect than a genuine hanging. Since it is presumably also more humane than a genuine hanging, it follows, by an exact analogue of Mill's argument for preferring hanging to imprisonment with hard labour, that faked execution should be preferred to real execution.

Mill's argument for the death penalty does not appear to be helped after all by his principle about apparent and real severity of punishment. So far as the practical power of punishment is concerned, appearance is everything; this makes it a question why, if all it is meant to do is deter, punishment cannot be purely apparent. There is perhaps a utilitarian answer to this question based on how the public welfare would be damaged if it ever came to be suspected that certain punishments were faked. There might be another answer based on the utility of making it a rule to tell the truth. But it is unclear whether utilitarians object to faking punishments, or only to being slack in keeping faked punishment secret.

Putting aside qualms about Mill's principle concerning

real and apparent severity, what are we to say about his argument for the relative mildness of the death penalty? The argument gains some of its force from describing execution as a 'short pang of rapid death'. Under this description execution may well seem to compare favourably with the lingering, tedious and arduous regime of life imprisonment with hard labour. However, Mill's line of though leaves out the finality of death. It insinuates that execution stands to life imprisonment with hard labour as a short, sharp shock stands to a long, dull pain. But the short, sharp shock is a short, sharp *end*: the alternative may be better just because it allows one to have a future.

Mill does not answer the objection just stated. But he does add to his argument for the relative mildness of capital punishment by calling into question the dreadfulness of death itself.

> Is it, indeed, so dreadful a thing to die? Has it not been from of old one chief part of a manly education to make us despise death – teaching us to account it, if an evil at all, by no means high in the lists of evils; at all events, as an inevitable one, and to hold, as it were, our lives in our hands, ready to be given or risked at any moment, for a sufficiently worthy object? I am sure that my hon. Friends know all this as well . . . but I cannot think that this is likely to be the effect of their teaching on the general mind. I cannot think that the cultivating of a peculiar sensitiveness of conscience on this one point, over and above what results from the general cultivation of our moral sentiments, is permanently consistent with assigning in our own minds to the fact of death no more than the degree of relative importance which belongs to it among other incidents of our humanity. The men of old cared too little about death, and gave their own lives or took those of others with equal recklessness. Our danger is of the opposite kind, lest we should be so much shocked by death, in general and in the abstract, as to care too much about it in individual cases, both those of other people and our own, which call for its being risked.[10]

Mill thinks that it is possible to care too much about preserving life and that this 'effeminacy' of attitude, as he calls it elsewhere in his speech, is encouraged by pleas for the total abolition of the death penalty. He himself seems to favour a mean of 'manliness' between the extremes of recklessness and timidity.

Misgivings are bound to be felt about Mill's use of the contrast between manliness and effeminacy. Let us take these as read, and consider other weaknesses of his argument. To begin with, it is hard to see why shock at another's death should discourage one from giving up one's own life for a worthy object. Is not the standard example of giving up one's own life for a worthy object precisely that of sacrificing one's life so that the life of another can be saved? And is this not a case that combines, if any does, shock at the prospect of another's loss of life with a willingness to risk one's own? Mill needs to show that concern over the worth of life breeds timidity, but the only plausible thesis in this area is that concern over one's *own* life breeds timidity.

Again, even if Mill is right to point out the dangers of being shocked by death, it is necessary to set alongside these the dangers of overpraising the life-risking gesture. Encouraging recklessness in a good cause is only one ill effect. Another is the revaluation of evil acts. Many of these, including murder and assault, risk the life of the wrongdoer, but the willingness to take the risk does not justify the rewards of the evil act where there are any or take away from the wrongness of the act where the risk has not paid off.

Sanctity of life

Capital punishment is often opposed on the ground that to inflict it is to deny the sanctity of life. Mill does not ignore this position but his argument against it is brief. He first insists that it is not human life itself that ought to be sacred to us but the human capacity for suffering.[11] Then he points out that on this understanding of what is sacred any punishment at all might be thought to be wrong, since any punishment, not just capital punishment, involves inflicting suffering. Mill invites us to imagine someone asking how we can teach people not to inflict suffering by ourselves inflicting suffering on them. He claims that there is a good answer to this question and that no inconsistency is really involved:

> I should answer – all of us would answer – that to deter by suffering from inflicting suffering is not only possible, but the very purpose of penal justice. Does fining a criminal show want of respect for property, or imprisoning him, for personal freedom? Just as unreasonable is it to think that to take the life of a man who has taken that of another is to show want of respect for human life. We show most emphatically our regard for it, by the adoption of the rule that he who violates that right in another forfeits it in himself, and that while no other crime that he can commit deprives him of his right to live, this shall.[12]

This is a sharply posed version of an argument already encountered in our review of the 1982 debate, and it has considerable force. It does not, however, answer the point that regard for human life would be even more emphatically shown if the right to life were considered impossible to forfeit.

Mill is again on weak ground when he takes up the objection to capital punishment from errors of justice. He says that the objection would be serious if the errors were other than extremely rare; but he does not explain why even one wrongful execution is not tragic enough and unjust enough to make the risk of another too great to run. Since it is possible for even normally adequate legal safeguards to let the innocent go to their deaths, it is not enough to say, as Mill does, that the principle of innocent until proven guilty will always or often enough save the day.

The strengths of Mill's position

Sometimes in philosophy unsound arguments are used to defend a position that is not itself unsound. I suggest that this is what happens in Mill's speech. The general position put forward – that people convicted of the most atrocious murders should be executed – has plenty of plausibility, for the punishment does seem to fit the crime, and only that crime is assigned that punishment. Mill did not want to undo the effects of previous philanthropy and introduce capital punishment for a whole host of crimes. On the contrary, he held explicitly that hanging was too severe for most offences, and in general that it was best to choose a punishment whose apparent severity exceeded its real severity. These views allowed Mill to combine selective philanthropy with a belief in the appropriateness of the death penalty to aggravated murder. When he went beyond this and claimed that capital punishment was a supreme deterrent, when he claimed that to balk at its use was to display or encourage effeminate attitudes, he left himself open to potent objections. He might have dropped these latter claims; in that case, however, his position would not have been so clearly recognizable as a utilitarian one.

2 GLOVER'S ABOLITIONIST LEANINGS

Jonathan Glover adopts what he calls a 'broadly utilitarian' approach to the death penalty[13] and concludes that on balance it is better *not* to have execution as a punishment – even for murder. In the course of his discussion he rejects or departs from a number of claims made in Mill's speech. He does not, however, seem to me to discredit Mill's contention that the death penalty ought to be retained for murders without extenuating circumstances.

Glover begins by pointing out disagreements he has with both a pure retributivist defence of the death penalty and an absolutist rejection of the death penalty. His reason for rejecting retributivism – interpreted to mean a belief in punishment based solely on the ground that the criminal deserves it – is that retributivism can demand the infliction of suffering to no real purpose. Glover has in mind Kant's form of retributivism, according to which even a civil society on the point of dissolution must execute the last prisoner languishing in prison, on pain otherwise of sharing in the guilt of condoning the murderer's crime. The good of not suffering 'blood-guiltiness' counts for Glover as a 'curiously metaphysical benefit' of carrying out the death sentence.

Though one can see what he means, I shall suggest later that there is more to be said for the Kantian view than

Glover allows. Glover does not claim that his complaint about its metaphysical character refutes retributivism, however, and so it is unnecessary to pursue the defence of retributivism now. Turning to the absolutist rejection of the death penalty, Glover sympathizes with the view that execution is cruel and unusual punishment, but he denies that capital punishment can be judged impermissible regardless of the number of lives it saves or the suffering it prevents. He writes, 'the view that some kinds of suffering are too great to impose, whatever their social utility, rules out the possibility of justifying them, however much more suffering they would prevent'.[14]

Maximization with scruples

The utilitarian view that Glover supports rests a great deal but not everything on suffering prevented or lives saved. It does not hold simply that capital punishment is justified if more people would be alive with it than without it. Numbers of lives saved are important, but so too are other things. Much importance, for example, is attached by Glover to considerations which support the absolutist rejection of capital punishment. Foremost among these considerations is the special horror of waiting to be killed:

> What seems peculiarly cruel and horrible about capital punishment is that the condemned man has the period of waiting, knowing how and when he is to be killed. Many of us would rather die suddenly than linger for weeks and months knowing we were fatally ill, and the condemned man's position is several degrees worse than that of the person given a few months to live by doctors. He has the additional horror of knowing exactly when he will die, and of knowing that his death will be in a ritualized killing by other people, symbolising his ultimate rejection by members of his community. The whole of his life may seem to have a different and horrible meaning when he sees it leading up to this end.[15]

Glover claims that all of this counts in favour of regarding execution as a cruel and unusual punishment. Further, 'the special horror of the period of waiting . . . is a powerful reason for thinking that an execution may actually cause more misery than a murder'.[16]

It is not obvious that the period before execution *has* to be horrible for the convict; but even if Glover's description is accurate, why should it provide a stronger case for abolishing the death penalty than for altering the quality and perhaps the length of the period leading up to execution? For example, why is it not an argument for more widely adopting legislation introduced in 1921 in the American state of Nevada, providing that 'a condemned person should be executed in his cell, while asleep and without any warning, with a dose of lethal gas'?[17] That provision, taken from a 'Humane Death Bill', presumably removes the discrepancy between the fatally ill person and the convict. It is also far less ritualized a method of killing than a public hanging or the use of the electric chair or gas chamber. As for the point that execution symbolizes the rejection of the criminal by the members of his community, why is this not equally true of a judge's sentencing someone to spend the rest of his life in prison?

What about Glover's conjecture that the horrors of the waiting period for the condemned prisoner are greater than the misery of murder? This is questionable on a number of grounds. First, it seems to rest on the unsubstantiated premise that murder is normally sudden, unexpected and quickly carried out. If, on the contrary, murder is usually excruciating and seems to the victim to last for ever, then the conjecture comes to nothing. Second, even if Glover is right and capital punishment does cause more misery in the sense of feelings of horror and pain to the one who undergoes it than murder, it can still be the case that murder does more harm. For presumably the victim of murder normally suffers the greater evil. He not only has his life taken away, but has it taken away arbitrarily, without being guilty of wrongdoing, and in the absence of the safeguards of due process often extended to the criminal. Of course, where people accused of crimes are given poor legal help or are tried under a system that affords little protection to those charged, for example a system that extracts confessions under torture, then the evils attending the process leading up to capital punishment may well be worse than many murders. But unless an innocent person is tried and executed, the evils in the two cases do not seem to be equal. An innocent person whose life is deliberately taken away suffers a greater evil than someone who is guilty and executed. Glover is able to minimize the difference between the two cases by taking into account only the mental states of those who undergo killing. Harm or evil undergone depends on other things besides.

Perhaps Glover can reply that while the victim of murder suffers the greater evil in some sense, it is not a greater evil in the utilitarian's sense, for in utilitarian terms it is the length and intensity of the ordeal that matters, and for someone condemned to death the ordeal can not only equal the murder victim's in intensity, it is also bound to be very much longer. This reply may be correct if the only form of utilitarianism in question is one geared to conscious states. But if desire-utilitarianism is also taken into account the matter is less clear. The victim of murder can be assumed to have many unsatisfied desires, such as the desire not to be murdered, not to be harmed for no reason, and some others that, in the condemned criminal, *are* satisfied. Since the frustrated and unsatisfied desires of the murder victim can outnumber those of the condemned person, it seems to be possible even in utilitarian terms that the murder victim suffers the greater evil.

Side-effects and the doubtfulness of deterrence

It is important to Glover's argument that the horror and cruelty of the death penalty be as great as he claims they are, for he wants to oppose the death penalty on utilitarian grounds, and in order to do that he must cite disutilities of execution that are weightier than the utility of execution's saving more lives than it takes away. I have already questioned his claim that the costs of life on death row normally exceed what the victim of murder has paid, and I have claimed that other objections of Glover's do not so much go against capital punishment as against certain methods of carrying it out. Doubts like these make it unclear where Glover will find the counter-balancing considerations he needs.

He does not look for such considerations only in the circumstances of those directly affected by capital punishment. He takes into account side-effects of various kinds which, when added to the misery of the condemned convict, may tip the balance against execution, even execution that saves more lives than it takes. Glover mentions the misery of relatives of condemned prisoners,[18] the harm done to those who carry out executions,[19] and the harm done more generally to society:

> When there is capital punishment, we are all involved in the horrible business of a long-premeditated killing, and most of us will in some degree share in the emotional response George Orwell had so strongly when he had to be present. It cannot be good for children at school to know that there is an execution at the prison down the road. And there is another bad effect, drily stated in the *Report of the Royal Commission on Capital Punishment*: 'No doubt the ambition that prompts an average of five applications a week for the post of hangman, and the craving that draws a crowd to the prison where a notorious murderer is being executed, reveal psychological qualities no state would wish to foster in its citizens.'[20]

These side-effects are not unimportant, but it is unclear that they all have very great weight. The first mentioned is tendentiously described. The description implies that society is cold-blooded to drag out the ordeal for so long, when in fact the length of the 'pre-meditation' is often determined by the length of time necessary for the appeal process to run its course. As for those who are keen to offer their services as executioners or who are keen to witness hangings, who is to say that they do not continue to exist, with the same appetites, even where there are no hangings?

Glover rounds off his discussion with a number of reflections on the supposed power of capital punishment to deter. He is sceptical about the value of the death penalty as a means of discouraging would-be murderers, and he finds inconclusive the evidence for its deterring political crimes by opposition groups. The question of whether capital punishment can prevent atrocities committed by governments or their agents Glover leaves undecided, but he leans toward the position that the adverse social effects of the death penalty cannot be outweighed by the very small probability that the death penalty will interfere with a policy of mass murder or some other outrage. Glover's scepticism about the deterrent effect of capital punishment seems to me to be well-founded, but since deterrence is not the only justification for the death penalty, deciding that it does not deter does not settle the matter.

The suspicion that the death penalty might be justifiable even if it does not deter is likely to be strongly felt in connection with Glover's category of 'political crimes by authorities'. In introducing his discussion of the right punishment for this sort of crime Glover mentions the execution of leading Nazis after the Nuremberg trials, and the execution of Eichmann after his trial in Jerusalem, only to dismiss the retributive justification for them:

> The justification usually advanced for these executions is retributive, and it is hard to imagine any more deserving candidates for the death penalty. But for those who do not consider retribution an acceptable aim of punishment, the question must be whether executing them made that kind of activity less likely to happen again in the future. For, if not, we have no answer to the question asked by Victor Gollancz at the end of the Eichmann trial: why should we think we improve the world by turning six million deaths into six million and one.[21]

Although it is indeed hard to see how the world is improved by adding to the number of deaths in it, it is perhaps not so difficult to understand how the world is improved by punishing the guilty for killing the innocent. There is an answer to Gollancz if adding to the number of deaths in the world is a means of punishing the guilty for killing the innocent, and if this is a lesser evil than either letting the guilty go scot-free or punishing them in a different way.

Another answer to Gollancz – one that is more in tune with utilitarianism – is to the effect that the gratification or relief produced by the execution of an Eichmann or a Hitler could well have outweighed the misery, if any, that the war criminals felt before and during their executions, and could have outweighed also the misery, if any, felt by relations of the condemned person. I say 'misery, if any' because some of the defendants at the Nuremberg trials were defiant and unrepentant to the end: perhaps they saw dying for their beliefs as a dignified conclusion to their lives. Perhaps for such people there was no misery in dying, especially in a ritualized killing: the ritual may have lent vividness to the illusion of dying in an honourable cause.[22] As for the relations of such criminals, I said 'their misery, if any' because not all of them can be assumed to have been saddened by their death. Dr Mengele's son, for example, apparently would have preferred to have had his father dead long before he drowned in South America.

Must a utilitarian accept that an execution is justified if the general gratification is very great or at any rate greater than the misery felt by the criminal and those who care about him? Perhaps not. A utilitarian could conceivably reply that there is more disutility in allowing people to be gratified by executions for atrocities than in not allowing the executions to take place. But if this is only a throwback to the thought that capital punishment strengthens the baser instincts of the public, the reply is not very compelling. It *may* be true that it is only out of a general bloodthirstiness that people have been gratified by the killing of a war criminal. But in circumstances in which people are publicly tried for atrocities and the evidence for the commission of the crime is uncontroversial, the guilt of the accused is a publicly available reason for the execution and for being gratified at the carrying out of the execution, even if what in fact produces the gratification is a wish to see someone's, anyone's, blood spilt. These reasons independent of bloodthirstiness are not touched by the utilitarian objection to gratifying bloodlust. So there may be an answer to Gollancz's question that is acceptable even from a utilitarian point of view.

3 GLOVER VERSUS MILL

Are Glover's abolitionist leanings more reasonable than Mill's retentionist ones? My view is that they are not. Too much of Glover's case depends on claims about the relative horrors of the death penalty that are not convincingly made out. And while he has valid misgivings about the argument from deterrence for capital punishment, he seems to me to have no compelling objections against other defences of the death penalty, in particular, no compelling objections to a retributivist case for execution in extreme cases. Mill's position also appeals because the arguments he gives for retaining a death penalty are not only to do with deterrence. He brings in the appropriateness of execution to certain offences. The argument from appropriateness, if it is not retributivist, is at least consistent with retributivism, and has whatever intuitive appeal attaches to punishing purely on account of guilt. By the same token, however, Mill's position is not a pure utilitarian defence of capital punishment. Its strictly utilitarian elements, namely its arguments from deterrence, are objectionable, in part for reasons given by Glover. The strength of Mill's case seems to lie precisely in its non-utilitarian elements.

Mill's and Glover's positions do not, of course, exhaust all possible utilitarian positions on capital punishment, and to the extent that my criticisms depend on points that are peculiar to their accounts, there is some justice in the complaint that I have not given utilitarianism a fair run for its money. On the other hand, I do not see how utilitarian arguments in favour of the death penalty can be completely detached from a deterrence argument, and it seems that no one knows how to make such an argument conclusive. As for utilitarian arguments against capital punishment, they face the difficulty of saying in utilitarian terms what is wrong with killing; to give the weight to killing that intuition does, believers in classical utilitarianism have to adopt supplementary principles with that effect.[23]

Modified utilitarian theories *are* able to weigh the direct and indirect disutility of killing and the misery of anticipation so as to tip the balance against the death penalty, but they seem unable to give sufficient weight to the enormity of murder, and to the compounded enormity of murder brutally carried out, as reasons for punishing murderers severely. Yet intuitively, brutality matters considerably in justifying the punishment of death. Now the departure of utilitarianism from intuition would not matter if utilitarianism were able to show why brutality did not really matter while acknowledging that it seemed to. However, the likely utilitarian explanation, that the brutal act happened in the past and the response to it must look to the future, that more happiness will be produced by overlooking or forgetting the brutality than by trying to get even for it – these reasons are not necessarily more convincing than the thought that only a severe punishment fits the crime, and that wrongs committed in the past are no less real for being behind us. The difficulty that the utilitarian has in denying that extreme crime deserves extreme punishment may be reflected in the periodic reawakening in Britain of retributivist sentiment against murderers, even though the moral climate in that country is overwhelmingly utilitarian.

NOTES

1 *Parliamentary Debates (Hansard)*, third series, 21 April 1868. Reprinted in Singer, P. (ed.) (1986) *Applied Ethics*, Oxford University Press, pp. 97–104. Page references are to Singer.
2 *Ibid.*, p. 98.
3 *Ibid.*, pp. 99–100.
4 *Ibid.*, p. 92.
5 *Ibid.*, p. 100.
6 *Ibid.*
7 *Ibid.*, p. 98.
8 *Ibid.*, p. 99.
9 *Ibid.*
10 *Ibid.*, p. 101.
11 *Ibid.*, p. 102.
12 *Ibid.*
13 Glover, Jonathan (1977) *Causing Death and Saving Lives*, Penguin, chapter 18.

14 *Ibid.*, p. 233.
15 *Ibid.*, pp. 231–2.
16 *Ibid.*, p. 233.
17 Bedau, Hugo Adam (ed.) (1982) *The Death Penalty in America*, Oxford University Press, p. 16.
18 Glover, *op. cit.*, pp. 233–4.
19 *Ibid.*, p. 234.
20 *Ibid.*, p. 235.
21 *Ibid.*, p. 243.
22 See Conot, Robert (1983) *Justice at Nuremberg*, Weidenfeld & Nicholson, on the reaction of Hans Frank, a Nazi administrator of occupied Poland, to the death sentence: 'Frank . . . was almost serene. Reading *The Song of Bernadette*, he identified himself with the martyrs of the Church . . .' (p. 502).
23 Such as Glover's autonomy principle, *op. cit.*, chapter 5.

CHAPTER FIVE

Cruel and unusual punishment?

Opponents of the death penalty sometimes argue for its abolition on the ground that it is cruel and unusual and therefore impermissible punishment. According to them, nothing that deprives a person of his life can be a usual punishment, and it is cruel for anyone to have his days ended by a period of waiting to be hanged, electrocuted or gassed. So however effective it is as a means of preventing crime, execution is wrong and must be avoided. This argument is non-utilitarian. In its most common form it claims that nothing can justify the premeditated killing that execution involves. It says that even when capital punishment prevents a greater evil it is itself too great an evil to be countenanced.

Other non-utilitarian arguments against the death penalty emphasize the risk of killing the innocent in error, the tradition of barbarous punishment that the death penalty prolongs, and the way in which execution pre-empts repentance on the part of the wrongdoer. Are any of these arguments to be preferred to Glover's case for abolition? I shall suggest that while at least one is stronger than Glover's, it is probably weaker than another non-utilitarian line of thought in *favour* of execution. The argument I have in mind leads to part of Mill's conclusion (that death is the appropriate penalty for aggravated murder) from premises suggested by Kant. It will be discussed later. In this chapter I consider only the case for abolition.

1 ON NOT TURNING BACK THE CLOCK

In some countries the abolition of capital punishment has been the culmination of hundreds of years of change in the system of criminal law. The change is naturally described as change for the better. Yet supporters of the reintroduction of capital punishment are committed to holding that the process of reform has gone too far, and that some of it must be undone. A brief survey of the historical record in European countries shows that it would be wrong to undo much of the reform. But how much is too much?

Idleness was a capital crime in ancient Athens, outlawed in the seventh century BC when Draco's code of law was in force. So Plutarch claims.[1] Again according to Plutarch death was the Draconian penalty for stealing fruit or salad. Under the law of Solon in the sixth century BC Athenians were liable to be executed for making misleading public speeches. In Rome, in the middle of the fifth century, an insolvent debtor with several creditors could lawfully be killed and have his body cut into pieces according to the amounts of the different creditors' claims. Thieves could be crucified. The criminal code of the Holy Roman Empire, still largely in force in Austria, Prussia and other German principalities in the sixteenth century, punished sorcery, arson, sodomy and counterfeiting by burning at the stake. Convicted blasphemers could be executed at a judge's discretion. Beheading was lawful punishment for getting involved in a major brawl.

In France before 1789 'the death penalty was implemented by hanging, beheading, burning at the stake, breaking on the wheel, or quartering, and corporal punishments included cutting off or burning the hand, cutting off the tongue, the mouth, and the ears'.[2] Capital crimes in England under the Tudors and Stuarts included vagrancy, heresy and witchcraft among, in all, about fifty kinds of offence. Hanging was the preferred method of execution but other more gruesome techniques were not unknown: for treason by a man the punishment could be drawing, hanging, disembowelling or quartering; poisoners were boiled to death. It was not until the end of the eighteenth century that the system of criminal law in Europe started to reflect in less severe penalties the ideas of Enlightenment reformers such as Beccaria.[3] For example, in the *Landrecht*, the code of law worked out in Prussia during the reign of Frederick the Great and enacted in 1794, imprisonment took the place of execution for many crimes that had previously been punishable by death. Later Prussian law took the process of reform still further: after 1857, capital punishment was reserved for treason, assault on the sovereign and various kinds of homicide.[4]

Britain was slow to reduce the number of crimes that attracted the death penalty: in 1819, 233 capital offences were estimated to be on the statute book, though of these a high proportion were for different versions of the same crime – forgery, for example. The accumulation of laws carrying the death penalty meant that 'the overwhelming majority of criminal offences were capital, irrespective of their gravity – from murder and high treason to pickpocketing of twelve pence or more, destroying trees and being in the company of gypsies'.[5] The severity of the penalty for so wide a range of crimes proved to be self-defeating. Convictions were often returned reluctantly and judges were lenient in interpreting capital statutes. A sentence of death was often commuted to one of transportation overseas. When the statutes were interpreted and applied strictly, it was for the purpose of deterring criminals by making an example of a particular culprit.

The number of capital crimes started to be reduced in the early nineteenth century. By 1841 only ten offences punishable by death were recognized, and in 1861 murder was the only crime that led routinely to execution, the remaining capital offences being restricted to exotic types of arson, piracy and treason. In the twentieth century, Bills for the abolition of capital punishment were introduced in 1924, 1925 and 1956. An Act that passed into law in 1957 restricted the kind of murder that could qualify as a capital offence, and in 1965 murder of any kind ceased to be punishable by death. (Treason, piracy and arson in naval shipyards seem to remain, in theory, capital offences.)[6]

It is natural to describe changes in the use of the death

penalty in Europe since the end of the eighteenth century as changes for the better. This description does not entail, however, that the total abolition of the death penalty in Britain was as much of an improvement on what went before it as, say, the abolition of death by boiling was on *its* antecedents. One could consistently hold, as Mill did in his speech of 1868, that while the trend of punishing crime less severely was admirable on the whole, it was possible for it to go too far, as when it involved dropping the death penalty for aggravated murder. Whether the total abolition of the death penalty improved on an already substantial record of penal reform or whether it exceeded the reasonable limits of such reform depends on the moral principles that explain why the general trend constituted progress. If the reasons why it was good to stop beheading people for brawling are also reasons why it was good to abolish the death penalty for murder, then the whole process of change in Britain up to 1965 may well have been change for the better. On the other hand, if a principle favouring the abolition of most capital offences does *not* extend to all, then the period of progress may end before 1965. In that case there may be a reason for undoing some of the reform, including, perhaps, the abolition of the death penalty for murder.

Is there a good reason for reverting to an older order, or is it more reasonable not to turn back the clock and to keep the ban on capital punishment? The abolitionist would have a strong case for maintaining the ban on the death penalty if the case for bringing it back denied the obvious, namely, that a great deal of progress has been made since the end of the eighteenth century. If it is part of the argument for execution that Draco had the right idea or that it is not too late to reintroduce boiling for poisoners,[7] then the case for execution is weak. In other words, no acceptable case for capital punishment can be a case for turning the clock all the way back. But perhaps any argument that justified execution would be an argument for turning the clock, if not all the way back, then too far back? I shall show that this conjecture is ill-founded. Arguments for the reintroduction of capital punishment can use principles that limit its use and that limit the employment of severe punishment generally.

Take first the argument that capital punishment ought to be reintroduced because it would deter would-be murderers. On a natural interpretation the argument assumes that capital punishment deters would-be murderers because they, like other people, do not want to die and are afraid that they would be caught and executed if they did kill someone. Let us accept this assumption and ask whether would-be murderers would not be all the more afraid and so all the more effectively deterred if they believed that they ran the risk of being burnt at the stake or boiled or drawn and quartered. It is hard for a believer in the deterrent effect of a relatively painless execution to deny the greater deterrent effect of an extremely painful execution. If the more effective the deterrent the better, why would not the argument support the return of aggravated capital punishment – boiling or drawing and quartering – rather than common or garden hanging?

The answer is that deterrence usually has the purpose of preventing more evil than it causes, ideally much more evil than it causes. Aggravated capital punishment, if it *is* more effective in deterring would-be murderers, is also the cause of more evil, which probably cancels its advantage over relatively painless execution. In other words, the thinking behind deterrence can be understood to have a built-in brake on increasing severity. Other arguments also tell against turning the clock back too far. Take retributivist arguments. Such arguments depend on the principle that the punishment should match or be proportional to the crime. Almost as a matter of the meanings of the terms this principle rules out a return to a time when the punishment was not equivalent to but harsher than the offence. So retributivist theories can favour reverting to an older order and yet have written into them a safeguard against reverting to *too* old an order.

Several arguments for capital punishment, then, can incorporate principles that prevent turning the clock back too far. So if there is something wrong with these arguments, something that makes an abolitionist position preferable, it cannot be that the arguments are too reactionary, but rather that the principles they use explain less well than rival abolitionist ones the progress there has been in the criminal law since the Enlightenment. Perhaps the progress does not consist in the gradual implementation of a policy of deterrence with lenience or a policy of retribution better and better proportioned to the crime. Perhaps the progress has consisted of gradually eliminating *cruel* punishment, where the threshold that has had to be exceeded for a punishment to count as cruel has gradually come down. On that view, the reintroduction of the death penalty even for aggravated murder could seem cruel – at any rate by the most enlightened measure of cruelty. In the next section we shall see how the objection that capital punishment is cruel has featured in a long-running legal controversy in the USA, a controversy that has influenced the status of capital punishment in law worldwide.

2 THE AMERICAN COURTS AND THE EIGHTH AMENDMENT

In America, especially in this century, judges have been among the most active participants in the moral debate about the death penalty. Partly this has been the result of a strategy followed by abolitionist lawyers in the USA in the 1960s. Gorecki describes how these lawyers proceeded.

> They appealed, with some success, every capital conviction. When unsuccessful on appeal, they asked for a writ of certiorari [a review by an upper court of a record of proceedings by a lower court]. If turned down by the Supreme Court, they petitioned the federal district court for a writ of habeas corpus [an order of a judicial inquiry concerning a prisoner's detention in custody]. If the petition was rejected, they appealed to a federal court of appeals, and whenever successful, they again sought a Supreme Court hearing. They also applied for post-conviction remedies to the state trial courts and courts of appeals with another potential resort to the Supreme Court of the United States. In this manner they aimed at reversing some [scheduled] executions and stalling all others, that is, at bringing about

> a *de facto* moratorium. They expected that once many hundreds of convicts were logjammed on death row, these convicts would be eventually spared by executive clemency if not by legislative action, since 'there were very few governors who wished to preside over mass executions'.[8]

Eventually the lives of many convicts *were* saved, but not in quite the way that the legal strategy foresaw. Sentences were not commuted on a large scale; instead, in 1972, a Supreme Court decision prevented the executions.

The Court issued a ruling in the case of *Furman v. Georgia*, having agreed to consider the question 'Does the imposition and carrying out of the death penalty [in *Furman* and two related cases] constitute cruel and unusual punishment in violation of the Eighth and Fourteenth Amendments [of the US Constitution]?'[9] In the Furman case the petitioner was sentenced to death for murder under a law in the State of Georgia. In the other two cases under consideration death sentences had followed convictions in Georgia and Texas for rape. In all three cases the Court held that the sentences did constitute cruel and unusual punishment.

Individual justices in the Supreme Court were far from agreeing with one another in their reasons for deciding *Furman* as they did, but an important consideration for many of them was the arbitrary and capricious character of decisions in which juries had so few guidelines to follow in reaching verdicts and judges so little guidance in passing sentence. The judgement in *Furman* and the language of the Eighth Amendment subsequently made an impact outside the United States. Amnesty International led a worldwide campaign for the abolition of the death penalty on the ground that it was 'cruel and unusual'.[10]

In the United States itself, the *Furman* decision was a turning point in a series of Supreme Court judgements which had fended off challenges on constitutional grounds to the permissibility of capital punishment. Hugo Adam Bedau has divided relevant Supreme Court decisions before 1972 into three categories:[11] those ruling that the introduction of a new method of execution, such as electrocution, was constitutional; those holding that the death penalty was not in violation of certain protections under the Fourteenth

Amendment; and those under which a challenge to the status of the death penalty under the Constitution was simply evaded. A notable case in the third category was that of *Boykin v. Alabama* in 1969. The Court heard for the first time the argument that execution violated the Eighth Amendment prohibition on cruel and unusual punishment.[12] The first real 'break with tradition', according to Bedau, came in 1970 with the consideration of the case of *Ralph v. Warden* by the federal Circuit Court of Appeal for the State of Maryland. In this case it was held that execution was a disproportionately severe punishment for a rape where the 'victim's life was neither taken nor endangered'. Being disproportionately severe, it was therefore also, according to the Court, cruel and unusual and thus unconstitutional punishment. A decision of the California Supreme Court along similar lines was handed down in 1972, just before *Furman*.[13]

Against this background it may seem that the *Furman* decision only extended an established trend of judicial opinion. In fact, however, consensus had yet to be achieved. Not only did the Supreme Court justices involved in the judgement disagree amongst themselves, but several states recoiled at the decision and proceeded to amend their legislation to circumvent it. This was despite the fact that only six years before the *Furman* decision, in 1966, public opinion polls in the USA had registered a solid majority in favour of abolition.[14] Again, between 1957 and 1965, six state legislatures had abolished the death penalty. Rates of execution had been in rapid decline anyway since 1947; the courts had simply lagged behind public opinion.

If the majority decision in *Furman* brought the law into line with the views of most Americans in 1972, it did so half-heartedly. Only two of the five judges who concurred in finding capital punishment cruel and unusual were openly abolitionist. The three other opinions in the majority left open the question of whether capital punishment was wrong in itself. As for the four justices who *disagreed* with the finding of the majority and found that the death penalty was not cruel and unusual within the meaning of the terms of the Constitution, at least one would have voted against capital punishment had he been a legislator, and another would have voted in favour for a small number of the most heinous crimes.

3 JUSTICE BRENNAN'S OPINION IN *FURMAN*

Justice William Brennan was one of the two abolitionists who concurred in the majority decision in *Furman*, and his written opinion is, from a philosopher's perspective, perhaps the most interesting of the nine submitted in the case. Hugo Bedau has described it as 'the most ambitious and sweeping [of the nine opinions] in its attempt to present an articulated philosophy of Eighth Amendment penal jurisprudence'.[15] At its centre is a test for determining whether a given punishment is cruel and unusual. There is a 'primary principle' presupposed by the test, which Brennan puts by saying that 'a punishment must not by its severity be degrading to human dignity'.[16] He gives as the clearest violation of this principle the infliction of torture. Brennan's test contains a reference to degrading severity in its first clause. The test as a whole is stated as follows:

> If a punishment is unusually severe, if there is a strong probability that it is inflicted arbitrarily, if it is substantially rejected by contemporary society, and if there is no reason to believe that it serves any penal purpose more effectively than some less severe punishment, then the continued infliction of that punishment violates the command of the clause that the State may not inflict inhuman and uncivilized punishments upon those convicted of crimes.[17]

Brennan goes on to argue that this test is passed in every respect by the death penalty.

The severe pain of execution

Brennan begins by noting that in the United States death has always been regarded as a punishment unlike others. It has provoked more debate than others, has been more continuously restricted than others, has always been treated as special by juries and courts. The reason the death penalty has been considered unique, Brennan claims, is that it is unusually severe, 'unusual in its pain, in its finality, and in its enormity. No other existing punishment is comparable to death in terms of physical and mental suffering'.[18]

Are Brennan's claims about the physical pain of capital punishment correct? The most commonly used method of execution in the USA as of 1980 was electrocution,[19] the painfulness of which is a matter of dispute. Execution by lethal gas and hanging, the second and third most popular methods, have also not been proved conclusively to be physically painful. It is known from the reports of eye-witnesses that the first execution by 'electric chair' in the USA, carried out in August 1890 with crude apparatus by a clumsy executioner, was little short of torture. But this does not seem to have been true of subsequent electrocutions. A few states in America employ firing squads and lethal injections instead of the more common methods, but these have sometimes been adopted because they are thought to bring death instantaneously. So it is unclear on what Brennan bases his claim that execution is physically painful.

What about the mental suffering of condemned prisoners? Though difficult to make precise, the claim that the suffering is considerable is not hard to believe. In *Slow Coming Dark*, a collection of interviews with men and women on 'death row' in America, Doug Magee describes the living conditions of people sentenced to be executed.

> Death row in most state prisons is aptly named. A set of small, one-person cells, segregated from the rest of the prison population in some way, the typical death row is just down the hall from the electric chair or the gas chamber.
>
> A death row cell is usually about six by nine feet and has three closed walls. The other, barred wall faces onto a corridor. A person inside a cell cannot see left or right of the cell. A mirror held outside the bars allows the inmate to see who is walking down the row. The room is ordinarily furnished like any other prison cell with a sink and open flush toilet, a cot and a light bulb. In some prisons the death row people are allowed their own televisions; in others there

are wall-mounted TVs outside the cells, always on. The rest of the furnishings depend on prison rules and inhabitants. I saw no cell that looked comfortable. One, furnished only with a toothbrush, was the bleakest room I've ever seen.

Death row inmates are treated differently from the rest of the prison population. They are constantly in their cells. They have no work assignments around the prison and have the most minimal shower and recreation periods. For four days a week, on average, they spend all but ten minutes a day in their cells. On each of the other three days they have an hour out for 'recreation', which is standing in a penned yard.

They are dependent on their guards for everything from food, toothpaste and stamps to communication with friends, family and lawyers. Because they are locked away with such totality they are virtually powerless to protest their conditions or even to make them known. . .

Death sentences used to be carried out in a matter of months after conviction. Now it takes years to execute someone who has been convicted and sentenced. Of course, the legal precautions causing this delay are absolutely necessary; and yet as a side effect they make the death sentence even more terrifying than it was intended to be. Life on death row is just barely living. It is instinctive existence where the days are stitched together by a thin thread of hope that either the laws under which the penalty was decreed will be ruled unconstitutional or one's conviction will be reversed for some reason. The effects of years of isolation and deprivation, the lack of human contact, touch and sexuality builds unrelievable pressures. The constant possibility of execution added to those pressures makes for a grinding, withering life that is all but intolerable – a 'slow coming dark'.[20]

Whether or not 'intolerable' is the right word, the conditions that Magee describes are certainly extremely unpleasant.

It is not always clear from Magee's interviews, however, that the prospect of execution added significantly to the unpleasantness that would have been experienced in any case. Several of the men who spoke to Magee were simply resigned to the electric chair or gas chamber or at least said that they were prepared for it. Some of them spoke of being unable to escape the memory of their crimes, and told how this soured even the grim experience of prison life. It is possible that years in prison without the prospect of execution but without the prospect of release either would have been more bearable: it is possible but not obvious. Perhaps what really makes death row miserable, or what contributes most of the misery, is life in prison rather than life in prison leading to execution. If so, then the mental suffering of condemned people is not necessarily a consequence of a sentence of death. Nor, by the same token, are conditions faced by prisoners on death row necessarily more severe than those of convicts sentenced to very long terms of imprisonment. Brennan's claims about the physical and mental suffering caused by a death sentence are thus disputable.

Brennan's position concerning severity of punishment is disputable in another way as well. For it questionably ties the conditions under which a punishment is too harsh to its being degrading or to its offending against human dignity. The fact is that impermissible severity and indignity can be independent of one another. A punishment that is unquestionably too severe, say being broken on the wheel, could conceivably be administered on the ground that it was honourable to suffer it willingly or without a struggle. One could imagine a military punishment along these lines, bound up with a military code of honour. Such a punishment could correctly be said to be cruel and unusual without its being true that it was degrading. Symmetrically a punishment that was degrading could be said to be mild just because it was not also physically painful. The shaving of heads of women who gave aid and comfort to Nazi soldiers in occupied France was milder than the slow execution of other collaborators. It follows that degradingness is neither necessary nor sufficient for excessively harsh punishment.

Arbitrariness and controversy

Brennan's test of cruel and unusual punishment brought in considerations besides that of severity. There was also arbitrariness: if a punishment was inflicted for some offences only occasionally, if it was usually omitted in favour of more lenient treatment, then the justification for inflicting it in other cases would be weak. It would seem arbitrary that the harsher punishment was ever inflicted. 'When the rate of infliction is at this low level,' Brennan wrote, 'it is highly implausible that only the worse criminals or the criminals who commit the worst crimes are selected for this punishment. No one has yet suggested a rational basis that could differentiate in those terms the few who die from the many who go to prison.'[21] If all Brennan means is that it is arbitrary for one person to be punished more severely than another for the same crime, his point is perfectly reasonable. But probably he is making the stronger claim that it is impossible to distinguish serious crimes by degrees of badness, so that punishing the supposedly more severe crime by the more severe punishment is always suspect. This claim is disputable because there are many specific crimes that can be distinguished as more or less serious. I take it as uncontroversial, for example, that someone who shoots another person intending only to wound the other person, but who kills by accident, is not guilty of an offence as serious as intentional mass-murder: the intentions and the numbers of lives lost make the difference. The same things tell in favour of inflicting the less severe punishment for the unintentional killing. Of course, it may be difficult to say *in general* when the more or less severe punishment is appropriately inflicted. It does not follow from this that the more severe punishment can only be inflicted arbitrarily or without a rational basis. This is to run together having a general reason and having a reason.

Brennan cited the controversy surrounding the death penalty in the USA as further evidence that it was considered cruel. The reason people disagreed about the rightness of execution, he claimed, was that the practice seemed to conflict with the high value otherwise placed in American society on human dignity. Brennan went further to suggest that in general, for Americans, it was no longer even an open question whether capital punishment was to be permitted: most people flatly doubted that it was right. 'The progressive decline in, and the current rarity of, the infliction of death demonstrate that our society seriously questions the appropriateness of this punishment today.'[22]

Excessive punishment

Brennan's final reason for thinking that capital punishment was cruel and unusual was that it was 'excessive in view of the purposes for which it is inflicted'. Whether it is meant as deterrence, as a means of expressing public outrage, or as a way of exacting retribution, Brennan argued, the death penalty goes too far. Nor is it true that no alternative is available: any purpose supposedly served by capital punishment is, according to Brennan, equally well served by long-term imprisonment.[23] However, his arguments in this connection are not uniformly compelling. For example, when he tried to show that life imprisonment is as effective a deterrent as capital punishment, he leaned heavily on the assumption that capital punishment had to be 'invariably and swiftly imposed'[24] if it was to deter at all. He then noted that under the American legal system neither condition was met, while 'the risk of long-term imprisonment is both near and great'. The swiftness of execution seems to be neither here nor there if one accepts Brennan's arguments about the awfulness of death. If death really is as terrible as Brennan and many others seem to assume, then it ought to deter even if it is not the criminal's immediate fate. And one would not have expected any punishment at all to be *invariably* imposed in a legal system with as many opportunities for appeal as the American one. Furthermore, the fact that the prospect of imprisonment is more certain than death does not mean that it is a better deterrent to the criminal, since it may seem bearable while death may not. Brennan is on even weaker ground in claiming that imprisonment can serve as effectively as execution for the expression of outrage at a heinous crime. This invites the protest, expressed by many who are in favour of the death penalty, that prison conditions are too good for villains who have murdered or violently assaulted the helpless and innocent. Arthur Lewis asked in the 1982 British Parliamentary debate, 'Why should we keep them in relative luxury in prison? I know, I have seen the prisons.'[25] The fact that it is far-fetched to say that prison conditions are relatively luxurious is beside the point. If Lewis and other people believed that imprisonment was too light a sentence, then imprisonment was simply not as good a way of expressing his and other people's outrage as execution. It may be, of course, that the expression of outrage is not a legitimate purpose of punishment, or that it is legitimate only when it is properly informed. That, however, was not Brennan's argument.

Suppose that life imprisonment and execution were equally good means of deterrence or of exacting retribution or of expressing condemnation: it still would not follow that the less severe punishment was the preferable one. If considerations such as efficiency and the cost in money of imprisonment are given significant weight the less severe may not be the best punishment. Nor is it necessarily a convincing answer to those who set great store by money cost and efficiency that some things, such as the saving of life, are more important than money and efficiency. For this provokes the reply that those guilty of extremely heinous crimes do not deserve to live, let alone at the state's expense.

Severity without loss of life

What about the assumption that incarceration is always a milder punishment than death? At least in Britain and America imprisonment used to be a far more unpleasant penalty than it now is, even when overcrowding and the sheer age and decay of some working gaols are taken into account. The facts concerning the old regime are worth considering because it puts in a new perspective the relative severity of execution and incarceration.

According to Amy Edwards's history of the prison system in England and Wales from 1878 to 1978, conditions in local gaols and the few purpose-built convict prisons were appalling until the 1860s. Dramatic reform had to await the review of local prisons by the Prison Commission under Sir Edmund du Cane. The new framework for prison administration, reflected in the Prisons Acts of 1865 and 1877, was accompanied by a new sort of prison life, intended to be 'as unpleasant as possible'.

> The resulting regime was indeed unpleasant. It was based on the principle of separate confinement, justified by the argument that an offender was more likely to see the error of his ways if left to contemplate his crime alone, with help from the prison staff and perhaps particularly the chaplain, than if he was allowed to associate with his fellows who would undoubtedly contaminate and corrupt him further. For the first month he was expected to sleep on a plank bed, and to work alone in his cell. The work would be tedious, unpleasant and as pointless as possible, and at this stage would usually consist of picking oakum. Later on, he might find himself working the crank or the treadwheel. Some cranks were small and were used in the cell, others were on a larger scale and needed several people to operate. However, prisoners working together on a crank or treadwheel were strictly forbidden to talk to each other. The food consisted basically of bread, meal and potatoes and was monotonous and unpalatable. No letters or visits were allowed for the first three months, and were then permitted only at three monthly intervals.[26]

Lewis's criticism of British prison conditions in 1982 cannot conceivably be made against the regime Edwards describes. And yet harsh as it is, the regime seems to escape at least one of Brennan's strictures on the death penalty. It does not have the finality of execution, or its enormity. It probably did not inspire as much controversy when in force as the seemingly more severe punishment of death. Edwards's report does not indicate that it was inflicted capriciously. And while it was probably more severe than it had to be for its intended purpose, namely, to deter and exact retribution for non-capital crimes, it would not strike everyone – it would not strike Lewis presumably – as excessive for the villains and criminals he thought should be 'put down' for their killing.

Though the old style of British imprisonment seems to escape Brennan's strictures, the old regime is not obviously superior to execution, at least when the latter takes place quickly and painlessly and only the guilty go through it. It may even be less humane (because of its duration) than the death penalty. Yet the conclusion Brennan reaches is that no punishment is as severe and inhuman as the penalty of death.

4 FROM *FURMAN* TO *GREGG V. GEORGIA*

Justice Brennan's was only one of nine opinions expressed by the Supreme Court as to whether the death penalty was cruel and unusual punishment. One other member of the Court, Justice Thurgood Marshall, held views similar to Brennan's but the three other supporters of the majority opinion stopped well short of endorsing an abolitionist position. Four other judges formed a dissenting minority, although some of these were personally opposed to the death penalty and would have voted against it if they had been legislators. In their role as judges the dissenters felt that they could only consider the permissibility of capital punishment in relation to the Eighth Amendment, not pronounce on its morality.

The dissenting faction in fact set the pattern for future judicial decisions that eventually minimized the effect of *Furman*. Chief Justice Burger, who wrote the leading opinion for the dissenters, made the point that at the time of the adoption of the Eighth Amendment in 1791, the intention was not to outlaw capital punishment, only torture. This was clear both from the records of the debates among the Founding Fathers and from the language of the American Constitution itself: amendments to the Constitution put restrictions on the procedures leading up to a lawful execution, but they plainly envisaged that these restrictions could be met and the death penalty duly carried out.

Burger then pointed out that in the 181 years since the adoption of the Eighth Amendment 'not a single decision of the Court has cast the slightest shadow of doubt on the constitutionality of capital punishment'.[27] On the contrary, an unbroken chain of decisions had affirmed the constitutionality of the death penalty. Furthermore, Burger argued, it was not for the courts but for legislatures to reflect any shift in the public attitude toward the cruelty of execution. Legislatures had in fact registered no such change of heart:

forty state statute books had provisions for capital punishment, and in the eleven years up to 1972, the US Federal Government itself 'on four occasions . . . added to the list of federal crimes punishable by death'.[28] Burger went on to claim that even without changes in statutes it was open to juries trying capital cases to reflect in their verdicts any community sentiment against the death penalty. This they had in fact done in many cases, refusing to return the harshest verdict open to them.

So much for Burger's reasons for denying that capital punishment was cruel and unusual within the meaning of the Eighth Amendment. More important, perhaps, was his statement of the conditions under which, after *Furman*, states could legally impose the death penalty. There were two ways in which he thought that this could be done. State legislatures could try to draft 'standards for juries and judge to follow in determining the sentence in capital cases' or else they could remove the discretion of judges and juries altogether and simply make the death sentence mandatory or automatic for certain specified crimes, thus eliminating the significant element of arbitrariness or randomness in sentencing that all of the supporters of the majority opinion in *Furman* had stressed. Burger doubted that satisfactory guidelines could be drafted and he had misgivings about mandatory sentences, commenting that he 'could more easily be persuaded that mandatory sentences of death, without the intervening and ameliorating impact of lay jurors, are so arbitrary and doctrinaire that they violate the Constitution'.[29]

The first significant test of the decision in *Furman* went against Burger's conjecture that mandatory sentences were in keeping with what the majority had decided. In 1976 mandatory sentences were held to conflict with *Furman* in two Supreme Court cases, *Woodson v. N. Carolina* and *Roberts v. Louisiana*. But in a near-simultaneous decision on three cases brought to it on appeal, the Court found that new death penalty statutes in Georgia, Texas and Florida were acceptable. In one of these cases, *Gregg v. Georgia*, the Court had to consider the constitutionality of a death sentence on someone convicted of murder and robbery. The defendant, Gregg, shot and killed the driver and passenger of a car that had stopped for him while he was hitch-hiking. He took their valuables and made off with the car.[30] The Georgia statute that applied in the *Gregg* case provided for either capital punishment or life imprisonment, with the choice being left to the judge and jury in the light of mitigating or aggravating circumstances. The Court's judgement that this statute was constitutional is perhaps surprising, since the statute restored to judges and juries the discretion that had been found objectionable by the majority in *Furman*. It is true that after *Furman* a list of aggravating circumstances was actually written into the statute itself, but the list was worded vaguely enough to give judges and juries considerable and perhaps questionable latitude in trying the case before them. Texas and Florida statutes similar to Georgia's were found acceptable by the Court at the same time as they decided *Gregg*.

5 OTHER ARGUMENTS

Though it did not alter judicial practice very much in the long run, the majority opinion in *Furman* was an important contribution to the moral debate about capital punishment. It was important, first of all, because it spared the lives of so many prisoners who were headed for the electric chair or the gas chamber. It was important also because the arguments supporting the opinion ran contrary to the utilitarian bias of much of the previous debate. Whatever their failings as components of a sound test of cruel and unusual punishment, Brennan's principles about the severity and degradation, about arbitrariness, and about means appropriate to the purpose of punishment are not open to the objections invited by utilitarian views about punishment.

Judicial error and equal representation

There are other non-utilitarian arguments against the death penalty, however, and it is time to consider these. One argument that I have yet to consider in detail has to do with the possibility of executing someone who has been convicted in error. This was a danger touched upon by several speakers in the British Parliamentary debate in 1982, and it is regularly mentioned by abolitionists in America as well. In America, however, it is often considered together with the difficulties experienced by racial minorities in getting adequate legal representation and a fair hearing in American courts. According to one view it is because the poor and the minorities have had bad legal help, and because they have been despised in advance by juries, or because of both things, that they have been sentenced to death in error.

It is hard to be sure how many people in either Britain or America have been executed for crimes they did not commit. Some of the best-discussed cases of apparently wrongful execution, such as those of Timothy Evans in Britain, or the Rosenbergs in the USA, remain controversial. Still, a number of authentic American examples seem to have been discovered by an independent researcher in Alabama called Watt Espy. Some of Espy's findings were presented in 1979 to the Alabama State Senate in the course of their review of capital punishment in that state.

In his testimony, Espy cited the case of Jack O'Neill, who was hanged in Greenfield, Massachusetts in January 1898 for a rape and murder that had occurred the preceding year. The Irish were unpopular and O'Neill was a victim of the prejudice against them. According to Espy, O'Neill predicted that those who watched him hang would live to see his innocence proved. Shortly afterwards a soldier admitted to the murder and rape, giving details of what happened that only the killer could have known. Another case, from 1806, concerned the shooting of Jesse Wood. One of his two sons was convicted and executed but the other later confessed.[31]

In a number of other well-documented cases people have been wrongly sentenced to death but have escaped execution. Anthony Amsterdam, an abolitionist lawyer well-known in America, gives the example of two black men, Freddie Lee Pitts and Wilbert Lee, who were twice tried and sentenced to death, and who spent twelve years on death row for a murder committed by someone else.[32] In Britain there is the case of Oscar Slater, who was sentenced to death in 1909 by a Scottish court for the murder and robbery of an old lady in Glasgow. It took nearly twenty years for the verdict to be quashed.[33]

What do cases like these show? That the possibility of error always attends the death sentence? That errors actually occur often enough to cast the death sentence into doubt? It might be thought that unless conclusions of this strength are warranted the mere possibility of error is not a strong argument against the death penalty. In fact, however, this may be too complacent to be plausible. If a small probability of a small evil attends a given course of action, then, no doubt, that course of action is permissible other things being equal. Similarly, if a big probability of a big evil attends a course of action and one knows that it does, it seems correct to say that the action is *not* permissible other things being equal. In between these extremes things are not so clear. An action may or may not be permissible if there is a big probability that a small evil will result or, as in the case of executing the innocent, a small probability that a big evil will result. Capital punishment may not be permissible if one accepts the maxim of prudence, 'Expect the worst'.

A parallel may make the position clearer. Many people are convinced that while the probability of nuclear contamination by reactors is relatively small, the evil of it is so big that no more nuclear reactors should be built. A parallel argument to do with the killing of the innocent where there is capital punishment is no less plausible. But whether either argument is very compelling, or whether the maxim of prudence associated with it is, is another matter.

The abolitionist argument is unanswerable if there are factors apart from human fallibility that interfere with reaching correct verdicts or sentences. Such factors exist if, say, many potential jurors in a given jurisdiction are racially prejudiced and those who suffer the prejudice are often in the dock. Such factors also exist if the prevailing legal system presumes guilt in the accused, if it punishes offences not specified in the code of law, if it makes no distinction between those who are sane and those who are insane, and so on.

Now there appears to be evidence that racial prejudice has influenced verdicts, sentences and the rate of execution in American capital cases. Watt Espy, the researcher who documented cases of wrongful hanging, told the Alabama legislature in 1979:

> With but a few exceptions, members of minorities, the poor, the friendless, the uneducated and, if you will pardon the expression, 'the different' are the ones who pay with their lives for their crimes.
>
> The black man who killed the white man has always been more likely to pay with his life than the white man who has killed the black man . . . In my research, that is in over 11,000 cases, I can only recall two where white men were hanged for murders of black men. One occurred in . . . Georgia in the 1870s and the other in . . . Mississippi in the 1890s. Both of these white men were more or less outcasts, thoroughly despised by their white neighbours, one because he was a gambler and whiskey dealer, the other because he was considered a rogue in general, and both because they chose blacks for their closest friends.[34]

Research presented to the hearings of an American government committee in 1972 showed that a disproportionate number of blacks were sentenced to death in six states in the American South. 'Among 1265 cases in which the race of the defendant and the sentence are known, nearly seven times as many blacks were sentenced to death as were whites. Among the 823 blacks convicted of rape, 110, or thirteen per cent, were sentenced to death; among the 442 whites convicted of rape, only nine, or two per cent, were sentenced to death. The statistical probability that such a disproportionate number of blacks could be sentenced to death by chance alone is less than one in a thousand.'[35] Clearly there is a strong argument for keeping the power to inflict the death penalty out of the hands of racially prejudiced judges and juries, or judges and juries who are more likely to execute a poor defendant than a rich one. But unless many judges and juries are racially prejudiced or inclined to be harsh with the poor and lenient with the rich, the strong argument is not a conclusive argument for the abolition of the death penalty.

Some Christian scruples

A number of articles of Christian doctrine provide non-utilitarian arguments against capital punishment. One such point of doctrine, formulated by Canon E. F. Carpenter, is similar to the thinking in Justice Brennan's opinion in *Furman*. It is to do with the way in which capital punishment denies the supreme value of the individual human life. How it does this, in Canon Carpenter's opinion, is by sacrificing the condemned individual for the sake of the group. 'It treats one man merely as a means to another's end: it gives to society total rights over him.'[36] The sense in which the condemned man is supposed to be 'treated merely as a means' by society is not altogether clear. It is true that when capital punishment is inflicted on someone to deter others, the person is used to give warning to the rest of society. Or it may be that in execution one person is treated as a means of gratifying other people's appetite for revenge. On the other hand, it may be that the solemn execution of someone acknowledges, among other things, the condemned person's responsibility for wrongdoing and to that extent shows greater respect for persons than a regime under which there is no capital punishment and every killing is seen as the unfortunate and inevitable product of social and economic factors that the murderers themselves have no control over.[37] Carpenter himself speaks of the way that society contributes to the wrongdoing the criminal does.[38]

Two other Christian objections to capital punishment mentioned by Carpenter are its defeatism and its arrogance. Capital punishment is defeatist because it shows that society is prepared to make no allowance for a saving change of heart on the part of the people condemned. According to Carpenter each prisoner guilty of a capital crime constitutes a God-given challenge to society to help her or him toward redemption, and to refuse this challenge by resorting to the hangman is a kind of impiety.[39] It 'writes off not only man but God'. Carpenter adds that when people take it upon themselves to go through with an execution they invade 'the sovereignty of God', for by inflicting so absolute a punishment they display a confidence in their judgement that no properly God-fearing judge of another person could enjoy,[40] not even a British Home Secretary.

When Carpenter speaks of the 'absolute nature of the punishment which death involves' he cannot mean, presumably, the finalty of death, for that is no part of Christian doctrine. He seems to mean the failure to make any allowance for error and the failure to look charitably for mitigating circumstances surrounding the offence and excusing factors in the criminal's history. The idea that great weight ought to be given to these things is attractive, but also compatible with carrying out the death penalty in extreme cases where the factors are looked for but not found. To deny that these things are compatible, to say that anyone who is prepared to pass the death sentence has *eo ipso* not thought seriously enough about possible error or charitably enough about the wrongdoer or his circumstances, is to beg the question.

Another Christian critic of the death penalty, John Yoder, lays stress on a particular interpretation of the sanctity of life. 'To sanctify means to set apart as belonging to God alone, and that is what the Bible says about human life: it is not ours to take.'[41] Yoder goes on to contrast Old and New Testament views about the sanctity of life.

> In the Old Testament life was sacred – except for that of the murderer and the enemy. By trading places with the guilty and with his enemies, by dying in a murderer's stead (Barabas), and by teaching us that there is no moral difference between friend and enemy as far as their claim on our love is concerned, Jesus closed the loophole.[42]

Here is the sticking point, for it is a question whether this loophole *can* be closed. It is true that out of a wish to follow Christ's example one could choose to overlook the difference between friend and enemy and treat them as if they each had a claim on our love. What is implausible is that there is *no* moral difference to overlook, that murderers and enemies have as much claim on our love as friends.

If the alternative to regarding all lives as sacred is to regard all but the lives of murderers as sacred there can still be a very inclusive fellow-feeling. Yet Yoder seems to think that if the line is drawn close to where the Old Testament draws it, there is more scope for vengeance than there needs to be. As he interprets it, the Old Testment moves in the direction of outlawing human vengeance but it is left to the New Testament, for example Romans 12:19–21, to declare it beyond the pale. I can see that putting things as the Old Testament does gives scope for retaliation. What is unclear, for the reason just given, is that it gives *too* much scope for retaliation.

NOTES

1 *Plutarch's Lives* quoted in Gorecki, Jan (1983) *Capital Punishment: Criminal Law and Social Evolution*, Columbia University Press, p. 39.
2 Gorecki, *op. cit.*, p. 53.
3 For a general account of developments in this period, see Weisser, M. (1979) *Crime and Punishment in Early Modern Europe*, Harvester, chapter 6.
4 Gorecki, *op. cit.*, p. 60.
5 *Ibid.*
6 Blom-Cooper, L., 'Good Moral Reasons', in *The Hanging Question, op. cit.*, p. 122.
7 Or immediate castration for attempted rape, as was suggested by a constituent of Charles Irving in a letter quoted during the capital punishment debate in 1982. See *loc. cit.*, p. 339, col. 650.
8 Gorecki, *op. cit.*, p. 92.
9 The Eighth Amendment reads as follows: 'Excessive bail shall not be required, nor excessive fines imposed, nor cruel and unusual punishments inflicted'. The Fourteenth Amendment has five sections, only the first of which seems to have been relevant to *Furman*. Part of this section holds that

> no State [of the United States] shall make or enforce any law which shall abridge the privileges or immunities of citizens of the United States; nor shall any State deprive any person of life, liberty, or property, without due process of law; nor deny to any person within its jurisdiction the equal protection of the laws.

10 For a summary of the position advocated by Amnesty and other international human rights bodies, see the text of UN resolution 32/61, which they supported. The text appears as

Appendix G in the *Report of the Amnesty International Conference on the Death Penalty*, London 1978.

11 Bedau, *op. cit.*, p. 248.
12 Gorecki, *op. cit.*, p. 95.
13 Bedau, *ibid.*
14 Gorecki, *op. cit.*, pp. 90–1. In 1981 American poll findings were very different. A Gallup poll showed 66.25 per cent in favour of, and only 25 per cent against, capital punishment for murder.
15 Bedau, *op. cit.*, p. 254. Quotations from Justice Brennan's opinion are taken from the excerpts reprinted in Bedau, *op. cit.*, pp. 256–64.
16 *Ibid.*, p. 257.
17 *Ibid.*, pp. 257–8.
18 *Ibid.*, p. 258.
19 See Table 2–1–1 in Bedau, *op. cit.*, pp. 32–5.
20 Magee, Doug (1982) *Slow Coming Dark*, Quartet Books, pp. 4–6.
21 Brennan in Bedau, *op. cit.*, p. 260.
22 *Ibid.*, p. 261.
23 *Ibid.*, p. 262.
24 *Ibid.*, p. 261.
25 *Loc. cit.*, p. 345, col. 661.
26 Edwards, Amy (1978) *The Prison System in England and Wales, 1878–1978*, HMSO, p. 2.
27 Bedau, *op. cit.*, pp. 266–7.
28 *Ibid.*, p. 267.
29 Bedau, *op. cit.*, p. 270.
30 Gorecki, *op. cit.*, p. 25.
31 Espy's testimony is cited in Magee, *op. cit.*, pp. 167–8.
32 Amsterdam, Anthony G., 'Capital Punishment', reprinted in Bedau, *op. cit.*, p. 349; see pp. 234–40 for more cases of wrongful conviction and execution.
33 For details of the Slater case, see William Roughead's account in Hodge, H. and T. (eds) (1984) *Famous Trials*, Penguin Books.
34 Espy in Magee, *op. cit.*, pp. 172–3.
35 Wolfgang, M. and Reidel, M., 'Racial Discrimination, Rape and the Death Penalty', excerpted in Bedau, *op. cit.*, pp. 194–205. The quotation is from p. 201.
36 Carpenter, *loc. cit.*, p. 35.
37 See Gorecki, *op. cit.*, pp. 98–9.
38 Carpenter, *loc. cit.*, p. 36.

39 *Ibid.*
40 *Ibid.*, p. 37.
41 Yoder, John Howard, 'A Christian Perspective', in Bedau, *op. cit.*, p. 371.
42 *Ibid.*, p. 371.

CHAPTER SIX

A Kantian approach

Non-utilitarian arguments against the death penalty often suggest that execution violates the humanity of the wrong-doer. In the preceding chapter I considered several such arguments and found none very compelling. For example, capital punishment was claimed by Justice Brennan to be physically and mentally painful to the point of being degrading, making it unfit even for murderers. It is unclear, however, that capital punishment must be very painful or that, whatever else is wrong with it, painful punishment is necessarily degrading. Other arguments, such as those of Canon Carpenter, were also supposed to reveal a tension between showing respect for human beings and putting them to death for serious crime. Canon Carpenter's case was weakened by the claim that criminals are only partly responsible for what they do: less than responsible people can have a strong claim on our benevolence but not on our respect.

The drawbacks of the Brennan/Carpenter approach emerge more clearly against the background of a certain non-utilitarian argument *in favour* of the death penalty. What this argument shows is that an exacting principle of humanity can be reconciled with a belief in capital punishment. The argument I have in mind is Kant's, with some revisions to meet incidental problems posed by some of its claims. After going through the general theory presupposed by the argument and then the argument itself, I shall consider what can be said on behalf of the retributivist principles of punishment that it assumes.

1 CRIME AND PUNISHMENT IN KANT'S CIVIL SOCIETY

Kant is in favour of capital punishment only within a properly constituted civil society or state. In one of his non-technical works he lists three principles on which such a state should be based:

1 The *freedom* of every member of society as a *human being*.
2 The *equality* of each with all others as *subject*.
3 The *independence* of each member of a commonwealth as a *citizen*.[1]

Enlarging on the first of these principles, Kant says that when political arrangements show due regard for freedom, no one 'can compel me to be happy in accordance with his conception of the welfare of others, for each may seek his happiness in whatever way he sees fit, so long as he does not infringe upon the freedom of others to pursue a similar end which can be reconciled with the freedom of everyone else within a workable general law – i.e. he must accord to others the same right as he enjoys himself'.[2] In other words whatever any one person decides to do in pursuit of his happiness cannot interfere with what people in general lawfully decide to do in pursuit of *their* happiness. A state which respects the principle of freedom for human beings 'restricts each individual's freedom so that it harmonizes with the freedom of everyone else (in so far as this is possible within the terms of a general law)'.[3] Briefly, free action is action permitted by rightful law. Kant denies that when action is constrained by law it is already unfree, for he thinks of rightful law as willingly imposed by members of a society on themselves.

In Chapter Three I tried to describe the kind of freedom or autonomy that Kant thinks is exercised in acting morally, and I suggested that the abstractness and other-worldliness of this autonomy might constitute an objection to Kant's normative ethics. Whether or not that suggestion is justified in connection with the notion of autonomy assumed in Kant's moral philosophy, it does not seem to fit the concept of freedom used in the principles of his politics. For as he makes clear, freedom in the political sphere is freedom of outward action, not of inner acts of will, and what outward freedom consists of is absence of interference from other agents, not exemption from empirical necessitation.

The second principle of a properly constituted state, according to Kant, is that of the equality of members of society as subjects. This is equality before the coercive power of the law.[4] Each person in the state is liable to be forcibly stopped if he interferes with someone else's plans, and he has the right to coerce others through the laws if he has suffered such interference himself. Another aspect of this equality is an entitlement 'to reach any degree of rank which a subject can earn through his talent, his industry and his good fortune'.[5] It is thus a breach of the principle of equality for someone who is otherwise fit for a post or rank to be kept out of it by another person who occupies it by hereditary privilege or by patronage alone.

Kant's principle of equality applies to subjects; his third principle applies to *citizens*, requiring that each in a society be independent. The difference between being a subject and being a citizen is the difference between merely being obliged to comply with a set of laws and having a hand in framing them. A citizen is someone who has the right to vote on legislation, and 'to be fit to vote, a person must have an independent position among the people. He must therefore be not just part of the Commonwealth but a member of it'.[6] In order to have an independent position among the people a citizen must not rely on anyone else for protection or act merely as another's personal servant.[7] Sometimes Kant holds that to qualify as a citizen one must have property adequate to earn a living,[8] where by 'property' he means not just land, but also a skill, trade, fine art or science.[9] There are places in Kant's writings where he restricts citizenship to adult males,[10] but this seems inessential, and in the *Metaphysics of Morals* he uses a different sort of definition which permits women to have the status of citizens, albeit 'passive citizens'.

Kant's theory distinguishes between the laws actually framed in a given society and a more basic but equally public law which 'defines for everyone that which is permitted and prohibited by right'. The basic public law, which is used to judge whether other laws are right or wrong, 'is called the original contract'.[11] This is the hypothetical agreement by which the people in the state can be understood to have voted to trade a fruitless type of freedom, freedom in the sense that each is a law unto himself, for freedom to do whatever is permitted by the general law.[12] In other words, the original contract is the means by which people can be conceived to have consented to the rule of law. It is no part of Kant's theory that at some time in the past the citizenry of a given state *actually* entered into an agreement with one another. The original contract is only a theoretical device that gives substance to the idea of rightful or just law; it founds the justice of a law on the *consent* of people who are subject to it. The way in which the original contract acts as a test of the moral acceptability of less basic laws is by means of the idea of a people's unanimous consent: if a given law is such that a whole people *could* agree to it, then it is just; if not, then it is unjust.[13]

Given a state with a set of just laws, Kant's theory envisages a right of punishment on the part of a ruler or governor against people who break the laws or commit crimes. In *The Metaphysics of Morals* he defines a crime as an infringement of the public law which renders the guilty person incapable of citizenship.[14] It is unclear from this formulation whether every illegal act is a crime and involves forfeiture of citizenship or whether this is so only for a sub-class of illegal acts.[15] In any case, it is crime that is rightfully punishable by whoever rules a state, not wrongdoing in general. Punishing is defined as inflicting pain for some crime.[16]

In outlining his theory of punishment Kant is careful to point out that he has in mind only the judicial kind, not the natural punishment sometimes included under 'poetic' justice. He conceives of judicial punishment as operating through a legal sentence declared by a state-appointed court or judge, the sentence being required to be in accordance with the verdict of a jury elected from the citizenry. Only 'the people, albeit through the representatives they have themselves appointed [i.e. the jury], can pass judgement upon anyone of their own number'.[17] The institutions of a judiciary distinct from the government, a jury system restraining the judiciary's acts, and public trials, are thus presupposed by Kant's theory.

When he comes to the principles that are supposed to guide the imposition of just punishments, Kant lays special stress on the 'law of retribution', according to which like is to be exchanged for like in matters of offence and penalty. How this law applies to particular offences is, he says, for a court, not for the injured person or an interested party, to decide.[18] As for the court, it imposes a penalty justly only if the reason for the penalty is the crime alone.[19] Extraneous considerations about the criminal should not affect either the decision to punish or the choice of a particular punishment.[20] Nor can arbitrary use be made of a criminal under the guise of punishment. Even if the criminal loses his citizenship by breaking the law, it does not thereupon become permissible for the authorities to do as they like with him: his 'inherent personality' rules out arbitrary and 'infamous' forms of treatment. Whatever is done with the criminal must be in accord with the public law concerning his crime; it must not depend on some other individual's private project. In other words, the criminal is still an object of respect and cannot be used by anyone else merely as a means. This restriction is in force as much when departures from the law would make things more pleasant for the criminal as when they would make them more painful. Kant is against any opportunistic departures from legally determined punishment, even when the opportunism is humane or done for the sake of the greatest happiness for the greatest number. His reason is that the penal law is a categorical imperative.[21] Among other things this means that the law is binding in *all* cases in which it applies, and that there is an obligation to follow it irrespective of whether anyone actually wants to.

At this point, however, a problem arises. For if the criminal is still a person, how can it be right to inflict pain on him at all, even by way of legal punishment? Kant has an understanding of crime that is supposed to justify inflicting pain on the criminal. According to his account,[22] it is wrong for one person to encroach upon anything that is guaranteed by the state under the social contract to be in the possession of another person. The 'possessions' wrongly encroached upon can include rights against persons, such as rights of non-interference.[23] The fact that such encroachment is wrong is a reason for trying to keep it from happening, interfering with it while it happens, and doing something to cancel it out or make up for it if it has already happened. All crime involves wrongful misappropriation or encroachment; so there is a reason for preventing, interfering with or effacing the crime. Kant says that the purpose of punishment implicit in his account is that of 'suppressing' the crime, and he adds that the only rule for suppressing the crime that can be discovered *a priori* is the law of retribution. He seems to hold also that this rule is followed and the crime 'suppressed' when the criminal 'draws the evil deed back to himself [as a punishment] and when he suffers that which according to the penal law . . . is the same as what he has inflicted on others'.[24]

If Kant is right the criminal pays for his crime by experiencing the pain he inflicted or a semblance of it. But how much is there to be said for this way of facing up to past wrongdoing? Why should not the criminal undergo instead a trial which leads him to recognize his wrongdoing and which produces in him the desire to atone for what he has done?[25] Part of the answer in Kant's theory is that painful penalties are specified in advance in the laws that the criminal breaks.[26] Presumably it would be wrong – ethically or morally wrong – for the painful penalties to be promised to lawbreakers and yet not be administered. As for whether there is a reason for laws to promise penalties to wrongdoers in the first place, Kant seems to think there is one, namely that any law must contain an incentive for complying with it and a disincentive for breaking it.[27] The incentive may simply be the need to do one's duty. But Kant holds that it can also consist in the 'pathological' pressures provided by threatened pain.[28] Can he consistently hold this, given his insistence on respect for persons? Does the threat of painful penalties not act on an agent by way of his feelings or inclinations, and does Kant not distinguish these from the agent's reason, which is what merits respect? The answer to both questions is 'Yes'. Would Kant's position not be more coherent, therefore, if it required that the law appeal to the agent's reason in order to win compliance?

The fact is that in Kant's theory the law *does* appeal to the agent's reason. Kant holds that there is always a duty to abide by a law and that this is part of what is recognized by reason when the content of the law is grasped. However, the recognition of duty may provide only a weak incentive for law-abidingness in people who are imperfectly rational. Hence the double appeal to reason *and* inclination. At least half of the appeal is fully in keeping with respect for persons considered as rational agents.

What about respect for persons in the form of respect for their autonomy? Is this catered for by Kant's theory? It is sometimes claimed that by threatening agents and providing them with coercive reasons for obeying the law one is violating their autonomy.[29] So must Kant not show that the state has 'a right to inflict suffering on offenders against their express will; and that punishment can be something other than an improperly manipulative attempt to prevent crime'?[30] The tension suggested in this challenge between respecting individual autonomy and doing something against an offender's express wishes does not arise in Kant's theory, since actions done against the agent's wishes are not necessarily violations of autonomy. For Kant an individual's autonomy is violated when an agent's activities in accordance with universal laws are interfered with. Now by definition a criminal's activities are not in accordance with universal laws. So the effect of putting a stop to them is not to interfere with the criminal's autonomy: it is to remove a hindrance to the genuine autonomy of other people.

Now it may be that Kant's sense of 'autonomy' is straitened and unacceptable. Whatever is wrong with it, however, it cannot be faulted for allowing interference with criminals. On the contrary, it is the inclination to *prohibit* such interference that is suspect. The inclination is encouraged by thinking of respect for autonomy as a matter of allowing each person to conduct himself by his own goals and values. The reasonableness of obeying this principle varies with the goals and values in question. In some cases it is flatly unreasonable to let someone else get on with his own project. For example, there would be a kind of contradiction in respecting the autonomy of someone whose goal was to deprive people of their autonomy. Or, to approach the matter from a different direction, if an agent were labouring under a mistaken belief, and the belief made the pursuit of a certain goal futile, that would be a reason for not pursuing the goal and thus for getting the agent not to pursue it. The same thing would be true if the goal were harmful to the agent or harmful to the agent and other people. The reason Kant's theory gives for interfering with criminals is that they do harm to agents who pursue lawful projects. Counteracting interference with lawful activity is in everyone's interest, since it maximizes the freedom each can have in the company of the rest. So interfering with criminals is in everyone's interest. This is not a consequentialist defence of interference with criminals: there is a conceptual connection between hindering hindrances to freedom and doing what morality requires; for by interfering with interferers one is promoting freedom, and, in Kant's theory, the concepts of free and right action are logically related.

Kant does not, then, put forward a theory of punishment which promotes the autonomy of the law-abiding at the cost of the autonomy of the criminal. On Kant's understanding of autonomy no such conflict arises. Nor is his theory of the criminal law open to the objection that by threatening to inflict punishment on law-breakers it fails to respect the persons threatened. Punishment *may* be threatened, because the persons addressed by the law are not perfectly rational.

2 KANT ON THE DEATH PENALTY

Kant suggests that in imposing specific punishments for specific crimes courts should be guided by the law of retribution, but he does not give many examples of the way in which this law pairs crimes with appropriate punishments. On the contrary, he implies that for many crimes a *range* of penalties can be appropriate. One of the few offences for which he thinks no such latitude is available is murder: for that crime, Kant claims, the only fitting punishment is death. As he puts it in *The Metaphysics of Morals*: if a wrongdoer

> has committed murder, he must *die*. In this case, no possible substitute can satisfy justice. For there is no *parallel* between death and even the most miserable life, so that there is no equality of crime and retribution unless the perpetrator is judicially put to death (at all events without any maltreatment which might make humanity an object of horror in the person of the sufferer).[31]

Kant is saying that nothing *more* than the death penalty (the death penalty plus some maltreatment) can fit the crime of murder, and also, more emphatically, that nothing *less* is appropriate.

The argument seems to lean heavily on the thought that the murderer must be paid back in kind. Kant thinks it is necessary to achieve what he calls an 'equality of crime and retribution'. How does he defend this requirement of 'equality'? As far as I know, Kant never explicitly argues for it. What he does instead is state a so-called 'principle of equality' which he seems to assume will be taken as self-evident.

> But what kind and what degree of punishment does public justice take as its principle and norm? None other than the principle of equality in the movement of the pointer of the scales of justice, the principle of not inclining to one side more than to the other. Thus any undeserved evil which you do to someone else among the people is an evil done to yourself. If you rob him, you rob yourself; if you slander him, you slander yourself; if you strike him, you strike yourself; and if you kill him, you kill yourself.[32]

Kant goes on to explain rather unsatisfactorily what he means by saying that 'if you rob him, you rob yourself', 'if you slander him, you slander yourself' and so on. He says that a robbery by one person makes the property of everyone else insecure. For the robber's punishment to make up for this he must not only lose everything he actually owns but be prevented from acquiring anything else. If in this dispossessed state he wishes to go on living, he must put even his labour at the disposal of the state. For a time he may even be enslaved. This account of what a person must pay for robbery is unconvincing because it seems to overdraw the crime. It is hard to agree that a typical act of robbery makes the property of everyone else insecure. Accordingly, it is hard to see a robber's losing all his property as a just punishment for his crime. In fixing the right penalty, much has to depend on what is stolen and why and from whom. The drawbacks of Kant's treatment of robbery should not, however, be allowed to discredit his principle of equality, which is indeed defensible.

The thinking behind it can perhaps be reconstructed as follows. When a crime is committed the criminal takes liberties that he has agreed not to take as a party to the social contract. That is, he does things that go against a law he consents to be limited by. Not only does he infringe laws to which he has willingly submitted, he acts at the expense of someone else – his victim – or perhaps at the expense of a number of other people. What justifies his being punished at all is the bare fact that he has violated a contractually fixed law or distribution of rights and duties; what justifies one punishment rather than another is the sort of violation and the kind of expense to the victims. According to the principle of equality the punishment should consist in a loss to the criminal equal to or in keeping with the loss to the victims; a relation other than equality would be arbitrary.

Equality can mean similarity of crime and punishment, but it need not mean exact similarity. Kant sometimes writes as if the criminal must not only be paid back but paid back with interest. Hence the penalty for robbery previously discussed. In that case the robber experiences an extreme version of his victim's loss, but he is not paying only for his robbing his victim: he is paying also for breaking the law.

Doubts are bound to be felt about Kant's insistence on similarity of crime and punishment. If the victim's loss was all that bad, surely it must be bad when the same loss is visited on the criminal. Yes and no. In some sense the criminal's loss is less than the victim's since the criminal suffers as the result of consenting to a law that prescribes that loss. What is more, the criminal cannot complain that when he suffers deprivation of property in return for robbery or indignity in return for indignity, he is worse off than the victim, for as far as possible it is the victim's loss that is coming home to roost. The criminal is directly responsible for that loss and indirectly responsible for the quality of a punishment that is similar to it. Another difference between the criminal's position and that of the victim is that the loss to the criminal is justly visited upon him. It would be a mistake to claim that on account of the similarity the punishment simply repeats the crime. What makes robbery a crime is its violating a law calculated to give everyone maximum freedom. The penalization of the robber violates no such law. So it is not true that the same crime is committed when the criminal is paid back in kind, for no crime is committed when the criminal is paid back in kind. It is not true either that the same wrong is repeated. The punished robber is not robbed, and the unpleasantness of losing his property is his due as someone subject to the coercive power of the law. So while he experiences unpleasant treatment, he is not wronged.

Kant's principle of equality between crime and punishment is thus justifiable, and when it is taken together with certain assumptions about the value of life and the harm involved in murder, the principle gives a reason for punishing murder with death. The assumptions are that life itself, whatever its quality, is a good, and that the harm in murder consists at least of the loss of this good to the victim. Taken together with the principle that the punishment imposed on the criminal should reflect the costs to the victim, these assumptions imply that the murderer should lose what the victim loses – he should die. I take it that this is the line of thought behind Kant's defence of the death penalty for murder. He says that 'there is no *parallel* between death and even the most miserable life, so that there is no equality of crime and punishment unless the perpetrator is judicially put to death'.

Now it is possible to question the assumption that life,

whatever its quality, is a good; it is therefore possible to take issue with Kant's defence of the death penalty. One could say that if the reduction in the quality of a murderer's life were very great a result of punishment, the murderer could experience a kind of living death. In that case the loss to the criminal could equal the loss to the victim without the criminal's having to lose his life. Suppose that this line of thought is correct and that punishments other than death do satisfy the principle of the equality of crime and retribution. This does not show that the penalty of death fails to satisfy the principle or that it is an unjust penalty for murder. The most that Kant has to concede is that death is not the *only* just penalty for murder. To show that death is not a just penalty at all, one would have to establish either that judicial execution involves a loss to the criminal greater than the loss to the victim, or that equality of crime and punishment is not as much a requirement of justice as the willingness to forgive or to be lenient in punishment. But it is not obvious that these claims are any easier to defend than Kant's.

Kant himself entertains and answers one objection in principle to imposing the death penalty for murder. This says that the death penalty is unjust in itself, because no one can be understood freely or willingly to let himself be killed. Kant attributes this objection to the eighteenth-century theorist of punishment, the Marchese di Beccaria. In reply, Kant holds, surely correctly, that what matters to the justice of a given punishment is not the consent to undergo it or the willingness to undergo it, but the free decision to do something that is against the law and that legally carries that punishment. The problem of being justly committed to letting oneself be killed does not arise. Indeed, it is not the same 'person' in Kant's technical sense of the term who on the one hand is party to the social contract and willingly consents to be bound by the law, and who on the other hand becomes liable to execution by breaking the law. For the criminal forfeits his civil personality when he violates the law.

I have been reading into Kant's argument for executing murderers certain assumptions about the good of life and the harm of murder. I have suggested that even if one of those assumptions – concerning the good of life – is dropped, the case for execution does not necessarily collapse. But how easy is it, in fact, to drop this assumption and hold that life is good only if its quality is good? Does this not imply that someone whose life is miserable loses little or nothing if he is murdered? Does it not imply that when the victim has his life taken away the loss is negligible, because, being miserable, the life was not worth having anyway? And is this implication not questionable? If so, the assumption that life itself is good may not be easy to dispense with. As for the other assumption I read into Kant's argument – that the harm of murder resides at least in its bringing about death – that seems very difficult to question. Given that Kant's defence of the death penalty for murder consists only of these assumptions and a defensible principle of equality of crime and punishment, it seems that the case is reasonable.

It is a reasonable defence of the death penalty, at any rate, where the crime is murder without extenuating circumstances. Kant's position is not so compelling in cases where factors seem to excuse or lessen the crime, cases which show that there are degrees of seriousness of murder. He seems to overlook the difference between a battered wife who deliberately and coolly kills her violent husband and someone like George Joseph Smith, who from 1910 to 1915 in the south of England drowned a succession of women whom he had bigamously married in order to collect their bank balances and the proceeds of insurance policies. There is also a difference between a robber who out of fear and nervousness fires on a witness, and Charles Manson, who is said to have cold-bloodedly supervised the ritual shooting, stabbing and clubbing of six people on two successive nights in Hollywood in 1969.

Kant himself says that where it does not apply automatically the death sentence ought to be pronounced in proportion to the inner malice of the offender,[33] but he never considers proportioning the penalty for murder to the malice of the offender, so that the nervous robber does not get the punishment of a Manson. He never considers proportioning the penalty to other extenuating factors, like provocation.

The classification of murders into those of first degree, second degree and so on is sometimes criticized as vague and arbitrary, but it makes an advance on the indiscriminate and unattractively harsh policy advocated in the *Metaphysics of Morals*. If there is any crime which the death penalty fits uncontroversially, it is more likely to be what Mill calls aggravated murder than murder plain and simple. Kant's theory is not changed drastically if one restricts the murders that automatically receive the death penalty to first degree or perhaps aggravated first degree murders. On the contrary, the restriction seems to be in the spirit of his admission that infanticide and killings in duels can only problematically be punished with death though they are arguably classified as murders.[34]

Though there are problems with making it automatically punishable by execution, murder is very plausibly said to deserve the death penalty if any crime does. Less acceptable is the classification of other offences as capital crimes, such as drug dealing and membership of a proscribed political party. Now Kant's theory envisages the infliction of capital punishment for crimes other than murder, for example participation in a rebellion against a government.[35] But it is unclear from *The Metaphysics of Morals* what the full range of capital crimes is supposed to be, and it is unclear why the crime of rebellion in particular should only be 'effaced' by death.

Kant does something to clarify the special status of rebellion in his essay 'Theory and Practice'. He writes there that the

> power of the state to put the law into effect is . . . irresistible, and no rightfully established commonwealth can exist without a force of this kind to suppress all internal resistance. For such resistance would be dictated by a maxim which, if it became general, would destroy the whole civil constitution and put an end to the only state in which men can possess rights.
>
> It thus follows that all resistance to the supreme legislative power, all incitement of the subjects to the violent expression of discontent, all defiance which breaks out into rebellion, is the greatest and most punishable crime in the commonwealth,

> for it destroys its very foundations. This prohibition is absolute.[36]

Rebellion is the 'greatest and most punishable crime' because it is the crime to end all crimes. It aims at destroying the state and therefore at ending the rule of law, without which the concept of a crime loses all application.

Even if we grant that this justifies Kant in calling rebellion the most punishable of crimes, it does not seem to justify him in assigning the death penalty to rebellion: the most punishable crime is not by that token the crime that may be punished in the most severe way possible. Kant himself seems to be uncertain whether capital punishment is always appropriate. When he considers the example of rebellion he admits that it is possible not only for death but also for penal servitude to be too harsh a penalty if the rebels are sufficiently honourable.[37] If only because the crucial principle of equality of crime and punishment applies uncertainly where crimes other than murder are claimed to be capital crimes, we ought to eliminate rebellion from Kant's list of crimes that can only be punished by death. One effect of revising Kant's theory in this way is to narrow down the class of capital crimes that it recognizes to that allowed for by Mill. Another effect is to give Kant's theory greater plausibility.

3 TAKING STOCK

A great strength of Kant's account of punishment in general and of his account of the death penalty in particular is that it is properly embedded within a theory of the just state and just institutions.[38] Kant does not suppose that it is possible to discuss the rights and wrongs of punishment without first asking how in general burdens (and benefits) in the state are to be distributed fairly. Whether his particular theory of the state and of just institutions is acceptable is of course another question: there are no doubt good reasons for disagreeing with the theory, and for revising his explanations of the principles of freedom, equality and independence. In connection with the principle of independence I have already noted some glaringly questionable assumptions about the dependence of women. Another objection, this time to Kant's principle of equality, is that it allows status to be determined by natural talent, which is as arbitrarily and unevenly distributed as advantages of wealth and high birth. Rawls's so-called Kantian theory builds in more thoroughgoingly egalitarian principles than Kant's own to overcome this problem. Again, it is possible to object to Kant's explanation of the principle of freedom – on the ground that it leaves too much room for the pursuit of the private good at the expense of the public. Finally, second thoughts are in order about Kant's test of the rightness or justice of laws. The test seems very permissive, counting as just or right whatever could *possibly* command unanimous public consent. Given appropriate assumptions about the relevant body of people, it is possible that everyone could consent to the killing of individuals who were not part of that body, or to the confiscation of the property of outsiders. Neither measure would necessarily be against the interests of sufficiently bloodthirsty or selfish citizens – but neither would be just.

Although these problems are not to be dismissed lightly, they seem only to affect the detail of Kant's theory. They do not seem to discredit just any theory that founds the justice of institutions on general consent, or that makes it necessary for a state to be well-constituted that its people be free, equal and independent. Different fillings-in of this general framework are possible. Kant's in *The Metaphysics of Morals* is one, Rawls's in *A Theory of Justice* is another, and there could be further variations. Kant's framework, in short, may well be robust enough to survive the rejection of the details of his account.

In the next chapter I shall not consider all of the points in Kant's politics which might be thought to require revision. I shall confine myself to those with a direct bearing on his views about capital punishment. Most of the outstanding problems in this connection stem from the retributivism of Kant's theory. Some problems afflict any version of retributivism, others afflict only Kant's. I shall suggest that many of these difficulties are less serious than they look. A theory that is both Kantian and retributivist is defensible even if it is not in the end completely trouble-free.

NOTES

1 Kant, Immanuel, 'On the Common Saying: "This May be True in Theory, but it Does not Apply in Practice"' (hereafter cited as 'Theory and Practice'), in Reiss, H. (ed.) and Nisbet, H. B. (trans.) (1970) *Kant's Political Writings*, Cambridge University Press, p. 74.
2 *Ibid.*
3 *Ibid.*, p. 73.
4 *Ibid.*, p. 75.
5 *Ibid.*
6 Kant, *The Metaphysics of Morals*, in Reiss and Nisbet, *op. cit.*, p. 139.
7 *Ibid.*, p. 140.
8 Kant, 'Theory and Practice', *loc. cit.*, p. 78.
9 *Ibid.*
10 *Ibid.*
11 *Ibid.*, p. 77.
12 Kant, *Metaphysics of Morals*, *loc. cit.*, p. 140.
13 Kant, 'Theory and Practice', *loc. cit.*, pp. 80–1.
14 Kant, *Metaphysics of Morals*, *loc. cit.*, p. 154.
15 In Part IV of the Introduction to *The Metaphysics of Morals*, Kant defines a crime as any intentional transgression of a law. The text of the Introduction is not included in Nisbet and Reiss, *op. cit.* See instead Ladd, John (trans.) (1965) *The Metaphysical Elements of Justice*, Bobbs-Merrill, p. 25.
16 Kant, *Metaphysics of Morals*, *loc. cit.*, p. 154. This definition commits Kant to holding, surely unnecessarily, that capital punishment is painful. Perhaps punishing is better defined as depriving someone of something for his crime. Further references to 'pain' should be interpreted in terms of deprivation.
17 *Ibid.*, p. 142.
18 *Ibid.*, p. 155.
19 *Ibid.*, p. 154.
20 *Ibid.*, p. 155.
21 *Ibid.*
22 My exposition draws not only on the section on punishment in *The Metaphysics of Morals* but also on Kant's remarks in

response to a published critical review of Part One of the work. See Ladd, *op. cit.*, pp. 131–3.

23 See Ladd's Introduction to *The Metaphysical Elements of Justice*, pp. xxii–xxiv.

24 *Ibid.*, p. 132.

25 See Duff, R. A. (1986) *Trials and Punishment*, Cambridge University Press, chapter 9.

26 General Introduction to *The Metaphysics of Morals*, *loc. cit.*, p. 19.

27 *Ibid.*, p. 18.

28 *Ibid.*, p. 19.

29 Duff, *op. cit.*, pp. 189–90.

30 *Ibid.*, p. 195.

31 Kant, *Metaphysics of Morals, loc. cit.*, p. 156.

32 *Ibid.*, p. 155.

33 *Ibid.*

34 *Ibid.*, p. 159.

35 *Ibid.*, p. 156.

36 Kant, 'Theory and Practice', *loc. cit.*, p. 81.

37 Kant, *Metaphysics of Morals, loc. cit.*, p. 157.

38 For the importance of political philosophy to a theory of punishment, see Honderich, Ted, 'Punishment, the New Retributivism, and Political Philosophy', in Phillips Griffiths, *op. cit.*, pp. 144ff.

CHAPTER SEVEN

Retributivism and Kant's retributivism

1 SOME PRINCIPLES

Retributivism can be understood as the conjunction of three related principles:[1]

The Principle of Responsibility: A person may be punished only if he has voluntarily done something wrong.

The Principle of Proportionality: The punishment must match, or be equivalent to, the wickedness of the offence.

The Principle of Just Requital: The justification for punishing persons is that the return of suffering for moral evil voluntarily done is itself just or morally good.

Or, to put the three principles together, punishment rightly involves paying back the offender, paying him back by making him suffer as the victim did.

Responsibility and the will

All three principles raise problems, but the Principle of Responsibility raises the deepest one. It can be put by asking whether there really are voluntary or free actions as opposed to causally determined ones. If the answer is that there only appear to be voluntary actions and that everything people do is in fact wholly determined by facts that do not essentially involve a will, then people cannot intelligibly be blamed or punished for what they do. And if conditions for punishment are not met, it cannot make much sense to ask how severe the punishment for a certain offence should be or whether it is right for offenders to be made to suffer. Important as it is, it is unclear that the problem bears specifically on a retributivist theory of punishment. Probably it faces any theory of punishment. As will emerge, some of the objections that can be made to the Principle of Just Requital are similar. They, too, call into question the whole practice of punishment rather than retributivist punishment.

Kant does not sidestep the problem of free will and determinism. On the contrary, in his moral philosophy he tries to make sense of the sort of will that can have effects in nature without being subject to natural laws. As already noted, the free or autonomous will that Kant tries to make intelligible is, in fact, not very easy to conceive. Kant himself confesses that it is beyond us to understand how the self-ruling will causes things to happen. Nevertheless, he does bring out a way of being subject to law that is not reducible to being subject to natural law, and in explaining why this unusual subjection should have more value than subjection to natural law, Kant helps, I believe, to induce the wish to be free of causal determination and to be subject only to one's own self-addressed universal laws. The wish to be free of causal determination does not of course make us free of such determination, but to the extent that we act out the effects of impersonal forces while wishing not to, our *will* escapes these impersonal forces even if our actions do not. So Kant manages not only to give us an inkling of autonomy in the abstract; he actually encourages consciousness of something like it in ourselves when we watch ourselves being the unwilling tools of factors outside our control. This account of the free will serves in Kant's system as background for his theory of punishment. So however slight a basis is provided in other retributivist theories for the Principle of Responsibility, Kant's gives it elaborate grounding.

Turning to the other principles of retributivism, we find them confronted with at least two difficulties. The first is that of determining what 'equivalent' or 'matching' penalties should be for the whole range of crimes. How, for example, is the rapist to be punished or the kidnapper? *Lex talionis* or the rule of giving an eye for an eye and a tooth for a tooth fails to suggest a clear course of action in these cases. The second and deeper difficulty is that even where an 'equivalent' or 'matching' penalty does suggest itself, it may seem wrong to inflict it: whatever suffering the criminal visited on his victim is still suffering when it is inflicted on the criminal himself, and the guilt of the criminal *may* not be enough to excuse his being made to undergo the suffering himself.

The Principle of Proportionality

The first of the two difficulties before us can, for convenience, be put in the form of a dilemma. Either the Principle of Proportionality is interpreted according to *lex talionis* or it is not. If it is, it is either strictly taken, with absurd results (e.g. should a rapist be punished by being raped? . . .) or it is taken loosely and found to be inapplicable altogether. On the other hand, if the principle 'is not interpreted according to *lex talionis* at all, it yields arbitrary results or it goes off into wholly non-retributive ideas about how punishments are to be deemed proportional to crimes'.[2] Since some penalties, for example fines, probably have an irremediably arbitrary aspect in that no good reason can be given for setting them slightly higher or lower, let us use 'arbitrary' as short for 'avoidably arbitrary' and read the dilemma accordingly. Then the right way out of the dilemma is to deny that the principle is to be interpreted according to *lex talionis*, and to deny also that in that case the principle yields arbitrary results.

What I am calling the right way out of the dilemma is also Kant's way. In *The Metaphysics of Morals* he says that it is sometimes impossible to exchange like for like in matters of punishment. He illustrates by indicating the way in which class differences interfere with applying the principle of retribution.

> [A] monetary fine on account of a verbal injury, for example, bears no relation to the actual offence, for anyone who has plenty of money could allow himself such an offence whenever he pleased. But the injured honour of one individual might well be closely matched by the wounded pride of the other, as would happen if the latter were compelled by judgement and right not only to apologize publicly, but also, let us say, to kiss the hand of the former, even though he were of lower station.[3]

He gives another example in which, without receiving violence for his own violence against an inferior citizen, a man of high rank had first to apologize and then to suffer painful solitary confinement. In this example, too, humiliation is supposed to counter-balance hurt honour.

Now even though Kant thinks that *lex talionis* cannot be adhered to strictly and even though he puts nothing definite in its place, that does not commit him to saying that retributive punishments must be assigned to crime arbitrarily or capriciously. The fact that there is no general rule for deciding on appropriate punishments does not mean that punishments decided upon cannot be appropriate. Perhaps there are some crimes so enormous that no punishment anyone could think of would fit – Nazi war crimes, for example. Still, in a wide range of cases, punishments *can* be appropriate, i.e. non-arbitrarily fixed. There is such a thing as using one's judgement successfully: when that happens the punishment is non-arbitrary *and* there is no rule that determines the punishment as the correct one. Kant seems to be illustrating the use of judgement when he gives examples of punishments for crimes involving members of different classes. Certainly it is a characteristically Kantian contention that judgement is needed in order to apply a rule or general statement.[4] *Lex talionis* is a case in point.

Because punishment does not have to be arbitrary in the absence of a general rule for assigning punishments,[5] the dilemma facing the Principle of Proportionality seems escapable. Taking seriously what is implied in Kant's practical philosophy we can say that good judgement is able to save us from arbitrariness where *lex talionis* fails to apply straightforwardly. Some considerations that might be brought to bear in exercising good judgement are mentioned in Kant's writings. To begin with, could the criminal complain that the punishment was too harsh without condemning his own treatment of the victim?[6] If he could complain without condemning himself, the punishment would be too severe. Again, could the victim complain that the criminal was being too leniently punished without the victim's presuming to be judge in his own cause?[7] If the complaint could be made without the presumption, then the punishment would be too lenient. Is it relatively easy, psychologically speaking, for people to comply with the particular law the criminal has broken? If so, then there is no reason for lenience.[8] Was the transgression unintentional and due to mere neglect, or premeditated and done in full knowledge of the legal penalties? If the former, then the agent's offence is minor, if the latter, the offence is significant.[9]

Now Kant seems to deny that in arriving at a suitable punishment for murder, good judgement is needed, for, as we have seen, he thinks that in this case *lex talionis* does apply straightforwardly.[10] I have already taken issue with Kant in this connection, suggesting that it is better to restrict capital punishment to aggravated murder. The reason behind this proposal is not that it is always a good idea to leave cases to be decided by good judgement, but that different murders seem to display different degrees of seriousness. A schedule of penalties which reflects such differences is not easy to deduce from a law of retribution, but it need not be arbitrary either.

Just Requital

Though it has no simple formula to rely on, a retributivist theory can, it seems, make the punishment fit the crime. What about the problem of justifying the return of suffering for suffering? Is is possible to provide a defence of the Principle of Just Requital? This principle holds that 'the justification for punishing persons is that the return of suffering for moral evil voluntarily done is itself just or morally good'. Bedau quotes H. L. A. Hart as saying that in this form the principle is extremely hard to justify, being no more than 'a mysterious moral alchemy in which the combination of the two evils of moral wickedness and suffering are transmuted into good'.[11] Yet, Bedau adds, the attempt to revise the principle so as to make it more defensible carries the risk of eliminating the most distinctive element of retributivism, namely its non-consequentialist, non-utilitarian rationale for punishment.

The first question to ask is whether the Principle of Just Requital really does make a good out of two evils.[12] It is not obvious that the answer is 'Yes', even if one concedes that moral wickedness is one evil and suffering another. For what is in question is whether moral wickedness and *suffering imposed on the wicked* are two evils. It is not obvious that suffering imposed on the wicked is evil even if suffering imposed on the innocent undoubtedly is. Indeed, it may be possible to give an account of wicked acts according to which no wrong is done in punishing them.

As we have seen, an account along roughly these lines is to be found in Kant. I say 'along roughly these lines' because in Kant's theory it is criminality – failure to comply with the public law in one's outward acts – that is liable to punishment, not the whole range of wicked acts, i.e. the whole range of wilful violations of the moral law. Criminal acts are wrong, according to Kant, because they encroach on rights allowed to citizens in the pursuit of their goals. The state and civil laws exist to secure the maximum scope for the pursuit of individual goals, the maximum scope compatible with harmony. Criminal acts unduly restrict the scope for the pursuit of goals by individuals. It is right for laws to prescribe punishments for crimes, since if the threat of punishment takes effect it interferes with the attempt to interfere with freedom, and so maximizes freedom. And if it is not wrong to threaten punishment it is not wrong to inflict it when the law has deliberately been broken.

To some extent a defence of the Principle of Just Requital is a defence of the practice of punishment itself. But the justifiability of punishment is not the only thing at issue. There is also the question of whether a wrong done in the past can give a sufficient reason for taking action against a criminal now. The issue is particularly delicate where the proposed punishment is very severe and no one, least of all the victim, will be in a position to benefit from its being inflicted. It is in this form that the issue confronts Kant, who insists that the execution of the last murderer should go ahead even if it is the final act of a civil society on the point of collapse or of voluntary dissolution:

> Even if a civil society were to dissolve itself with the consent of all its members (for example, if a people who inhabited an island decided to separate and disperse to other parts of the world), the last murderer in prison would first have to be executed in order that each should receive his just deserts and that the people should not bear the guilt of a capital crime through failing to insist on its punishment; for if they do not do so, they can be regarded as accomplices in the public violation of justice.[13]

As we saw in Chapter Four, Jonathan Glover objects to this position on the ground that it detaches the justification for the death penalty from any tangible benefits that it could bring anyone. Glover concedes that avoiding the guilt of condoning a murder could be an abstract or metaphysical sort of benefit, but he doubts that this sort of benefit really justifies the death penalty.

Glover's is a reasonable view to take of the case discussed by Kant. For in the circumstances that Kant imagines it does sound as if it is mainly for the sake of leaving no loose ends that one goes through with the execution of the last murderer. On further consideration, however, Kant's view may have more to recommend it. To begin with, even if no one benefits tangibly from the execution of the last murderer, there is a reason for executing him, namely that he willingly infringed a law carrying the death penalty and that he inflicted such and such a harm. This reason does not disappear just because the person under the sentence of death is the last murderer or because the state which carries out the punishment is about to dissolve. Although this reason for going through with the execution may not be decisive or overwhelming, the fact that there is a reason at all is enough to overturn the claim that the execution is pointless or that it leads to pointless suffering.[14] Indeed, the bigger the crime the less pointless the execution – even as a last act of a society about to dissolve.

A problem remains. When a criminal is made to suffer now for having inflicted suffering in the past, no allowance seems to be made for the possibility of an intervening change of heart on the part of the wrongdoer. Up to a point this problem can be met by Kant, for he distinguishes between motivation that would make someone an habitual criminal, and motivation that would lead someone only to commit the occasional offence.[15] Presumably this apparatus would lend itself to characterizing one kind of reform, namely the change from being an habitual criminal to being an occasional offender. And since Kant sometimes makes the infliction of capital punishment depend on the malice of the offender,[16] there is no reason why he could not make punishment in general proportional to the quality of the offender's motivation, change in its quality being reflected in changes in punishment.

Finally, how well does Kant handle the dilemma that was supposed to confront any supporter of the Principle of Just Requital? According to Bedau, the defender of the principle must either appeal to some independent good promoted by punishment in order to justify it, in which case retributivism is a consequentialist theory and not, as it must be to remain distinctive, a non-consequentialist one; or else an internal justification for punishment must be found, which may involve the alchemy of turning two evils into good. Kant expressly rejects a justification of punishment by appeal to its crime-preventing effects,[17] and he apparently repudiates the idea of punishing the agent for other beneficial effects it may have. The only justification he seems to recognize is the agent's commission of a crime.[18] Kant's justification of punishment is thus non-consequential.

2 KANT'S THEORY AND OTHERS

The central idea of Kant's theory of punishment is that by encroaching upon someone else's rights a criminal both goes back on an agreement to avoid certain actions and inflicts suffering; by being made to undergo comparable suffering himself the criminal effaces or makes up for his crime. In explaining why the infliction of suffering can be the appropriate response to a crime, Kant's theory combines elements of two present-day accounts of the significance of punishment. According to one account someone who breaks the law gains an advantage over the law-abiding. Either he gains property at the expense of those he deprives of it or he exercises freedom that others forego in being law-abiding. Punishment takes away or offsets the unfair advantage, and so restores a balance.[19] According to the second sort of account punishment aims to make the wrongdoer feel guilty for an offence, the pain of guilt being the kind of suffering an offence merits and also the kind that enables the criminal to expiate his crime.[20] Kant's theory can be understood to call for restoring a balance beween the 'possessions' of the criminal and victim in response to the criminal's creation of an imbalance. The criminal violates the rights of the victim and thereby inflicts suffering or harm. In return he undergoes comparable suffering but this time justly – without any violation of his rights, and therefore without any just resort to retribution himself. In a way, the criminal is disadvantaged more than the victim. He loses not only what the victim loses, but also something for being responsible for the victim's loss. Besides the suffering that the punishment itself involves, 'the sense of honour of the accused is rightfully hurt, because the imposition of punishment involves a purely one-sided use of coercion. As a result the dignity of a citizen . . . is . . . at least suspended, inasmuch as he is subjected to an external duty against which he . . . cannot bring any resistance'.[21] This loss of dignity counter-balances the indignity suffered – whatever the crime – by anyone who is a victim of a crime.

Though it is less clear, there are also elements in Kant's account of the expiation theory of punishment. Kant speaks of the criminal drawing the deed back on to himself as a punishment, and in one case of the infliction of capital punishment he speaks about a crime being 'effaced' or 'expiated' by death.[22] It may even be that for Kant expiating or effacing the crime is always the purpose of retribution. If so, it is clear that he thinks it takes more than the pain of guilt to expiate or efface most offences. So his is more severe an expiation theory than the present-day account that it broadly resembles.

Neither the mild expiation theory nor the theory that punishment restores a balance is on its own as attractive as a theory that takes elements from both. The restoring-the-balance theory fails to explain, for a sufficiently wide range of crimes, why the punishment is deserved. It fails to explain why punishment is merited for rape, for example. It implies that the rapist gets an unfair advantage by breaking the law against rape, an unfair advantage over the law-abiding, including the law-abiding victim. It implies that because of this unfair advantage a balance needs to be restored. But this is far less plausible an explanation than one that cites the injury to the victim of the act of rape itself.[23] The restoring-the-balance theory is better suited to saying why, for example, tax-evasion is a punishable offence. As for the mild expiation theory, it implies that the pain of remorse itself suffices as a punishment for a past misdeed. Perhaps the greatest difficulty with this theory is that it seems utterly inappropriate to the most serious crimes and atrocities. Could guilt or remorse by itself, even if very keenly felt, make amends for mass murder or prolonged torture or even a stubbornly maintained and harsh system of racial discrimination? To the extent that Kant's is an expiation theory it escapes these objections.

Some apparent problems

Kant's theory of punishment is an account of what may lawfully be done to criminals in the idealized setting of a just society. If no actual society meets Kant's specifications for a just society – if, for example, there is no society in which every citizen really can go as far as native talent and luck will allow[24] – then how can those who are arbitrarily held back be blamed, let alone punished, for trying to better their position illegally? Kant's theory does not justify punishments in unjust societies, and neo-Kantian theories[25]

justify no actual practice of punishment at all. Is it a good objection to either Kant's theory or a neo-Kantian one that it may not justify any punishments in societies as we know them?[26] No. All of these accounts suggest what practices of punishment there ought to be, and in doing so they set standards against which actual practices of punishment and actual political arrangements are to be judged. These theories, then, *apply* to actual practices and actual political arrangements, but without endorsing them.

It is sometimes claimed that an intelligible defence of retributivism must locate the justification for returning suffering for suffering in the satisfaction it gives to surviving victims and the wider public. These people feel grievances against doers of harm, and these grievances are fully assuaged only when the harmful agents are seen to suffer distress themselves.[27] The purpose of the criminal law, moreover, is precisely to afford means of evening the score with criminals. Sometimes this line of thought is summarized by quoting a Victorian judge, James Fitzjames Stephen, who said that the 'criminal law stands to the passion of revenge in the same relation as marriage to the sexual appetite'.[28] But how strong a justification for returning suffering for suffering *is* the fact that in a given case it would give to the victims and to society the revenge they want? Even if we grant that the existence of a want or desire is on its *own* some justification for satisfying it, it does not follow that it is a strong justification, let alone the moral justification that is in order when the truth of retributivism is at issue. Retributivism, by way of its Principle of Just Requital, says that it is *right* for suffering to be returned for suffering, that this is how things *ought* to be. It is surely inadequate to enlarge on this claim by saying that it is right if it would soothe feelings of grievance. If soothing feelings of grievance were sufficient justification for inflicting suffering, then suffering could rightly be inflicted on innocent people against whom there was a baseless grievance, contrary to a moral principle – against harming the innocent – considerably more evident than the Principle of Just Requital itself. Feelings of grievance, then, are not sufficient for the infliction of suffering, and it is questionable whether they are necessary.

Imagine the murder of a particularly despised person whose death inspired no grievance or wish for revenge. Would there be no reason in that case for capturing and imprisoning the murderer? Surely the reason for making murder a crime is some reason for punishing murderers, and surely the reason for making murder a crime can be the evil of violent loss of life, whether or not the violent loss of life is attended by feelings of grievance.

It is a merit of Kant's account that it does not mix up the justification for retribution with the satisfaction of the desire for revenge. Instead, it bases a principle like that of just requital directly on a conception of justice according to which the state guarantees to each what is his own and can call for the forfeiture of goods, including freedom, when state-guaranteed possessions are appropriated. Whatever the drawbacks of Kant's particular conception of justice, there can be no doubt that a defence of retribution that appeals to a conception of justice is to be preferred to one that invokes only the feelings of victims and the general public.

Berns's theory

At least one modern writer, Walter Berns,[29] has attempted to combine considerations of justice and considerations of feeling into a defence of retributivism in general and capital punishment in particular. He suggests that anger is founded on beliefs about the injustice of certain acts, that anger can be a justifiable reaction to these acts, and that when it is, the justification can transfer to *punishment* out of anger.

Berns's point that anger can be reasonable and that to act on anger need not be a kind of self-indulgence, is worth making against the well-entrenched point of view that morality and reason are generally at war with the emotions. Berns has a good point, too, when he notes that anger is properly directed only on to agents considered to be responsible and therefore considered to possess the dignity of responsibility.[30] This goes against the view that punishment inspired by anger is barbaric retaliation against the criminal which denies the criminal's dignity. Yet though he exposes certain misconceptions about anger and punishment out of anger, Berns does not seem to me to show that reference to anger is necessary in the justification of punishment.

Why cannot the injustice of the acts directly justify the punishment whether or not the acts make anyone angry? Berns's answer is that feelings experienced by people in a community make a difference to whether the community is a 'moral community'. A community is not moral if people fail to become angry at the unjust suffering of a member of the community. 'If men are not angry when someone else is robbed, raped or murdered, the implication is that no moral community exists, because those men do not care for anyone other than themselves'.[31] But this claim holds only if anger is the *sole* attitude appropriate to showing concern for others who have been injured. And this is far from plausible. Why could not pity or compassion be felt, for example, without anger coming into it at all? Not only does Berns fail to show that a capacity for properly directed anger is crucial to membership in a moral community; he fails even to acknowledge Kant's famous question of whether any emotion in the ordinary sense is necessary for obeying the moral law or (what is supposed to be equivalent for Kant) belonging to a realm of ends or moral community.

Kant has more than one argument for making a person's moral worth independent of his emotional capacities. On the one hand he thinks that the emotional capacities anyone has are the ones that a person has been given by nature, and that nature can be capricious or miserly in its gifts. If one is lucky one is able to feel a lot of compassion and sympathy; helping comes easily. If one is unlucky, on the other hand, it goes against the grain to make the kind or helpful gesture. Now if one's moral worth depended on one's feelings then the person who had to force himself to do the right thing would be less estimable than the man for whom it was effortless. This would mean that a natural advantage conferred a moral advantage, contrary to the thought that we should not get moral credit or discredit for what is independent of what we do.

A second argument of Kant's is based on the thought that actions inspired by the emotions are done in the pursuit of happiness and that happiness is too indefinite a goal to yield a clear difference between actions that are right and those that are wrong. Like Kant, Berns is dismissive of the utilitarian standard of right and wrong, but his doubts about it do not seem to go as deep as Kant's.

The main difficulty with Berns's position can conveniently be summed up by reference to a claim of his about the purpose of punishment. 'Punishment', he says, 'arises out of the demand for justice, and justice is demanded by angry, morally indignant men; its purpose is to satisfy the moral indignation that, it is assumed, accompanies it'.[32] Berns does not explain why the purpose of punishment should be to satisfy moral indignation rather than meet the demands of justice. Unless Berns thinks that to satisfy the demands of justice just *is* to meet the demands of moral indignation, which itself would require a considerable defence, he can reasonably be expected to indicate what is added to a demand for justice by the fact that the demand is made by angry men.

3 CONCLUSION

Retributivism in theory and practice

I have been arguing that retributivism is a morally defensible position and that Kant's writings contain the makings of an acceptable justification for it. Only 'the makings' of a satisfactory defence because I have found reason to depart from the detail of Kant's theory. Even in the revised form in which I have presented it his view of punishment is not completely without difficulties. After all that has been said many will still find it more obvious that the return of suffering for suffering is wrong than that extreme crimes deserve severe punishment. Even if this is so, I hope it will be conceded that Kant's theory gets round a considerable number of difficulties commonly thought to face the retributivist position, and that where troubles remain it indicates the type of *overall* account – a theory of the just society – in which these would have to be confronted.

It should be noted that the case for Kant's retributivism

does not consist merely of considerations reviewed in this and the last chapter. Criticisms of utilitarianism reviewed in Chapters Three and Four pushed us early on toward a non-utilitarian position, and weaknesses in the non-utilitarian case against capital punishment pushed us toward a non-utilitarian view like Kant's in particular. Whatever good reasons there may be for rejecting Kant's theory as I have revised it, they are unlikely to reinstate the accounts that it seemed to make an advance upon.

What if a Kantian retributivism is found compelling and his approach to capital punishment is considered broadly acceptable? How would the tenets of his theory be translated into practice? Plainly they do not justify those who have been criminally injured in doing whatever they think it takes to get even. Kant thinks that it is for a court to decide who is guilty and how the guilty should be punished, and also that it is for a suitable state official to inflict the punishment. Private settlings of scores, whether by individuals or vigilante groups, are not permitted by his account. What the theory *does* allow, indeed what it positively recommends, is the framing of penal statutes that make punishments 'equal' to offences, and in particular, that make death the penalty for murder. I have already suggested that it is unreasonable to make execution the automatic penalty for all kinds of murder. I have also pointed out a certain arbitrariness in Kant's choice of capital offences other than murder. The best way of coping with these difficulties is to narrow down the class of capital offences to the most serious murders.

Like the unrevised Kantian position, the more restricted one that I favour calls for the reintroduction of capital punishment statutes where they have been abolished and the maintenance of them where they are in place. But is this a workable recommendation? In the case of *McGautha v. California* in 1971, Justice John Marshall Harlan wrote that those

> who have come to grips with the hard task of actually attempting to draft means of channelling capital sentencing discretion have confirmed the lesson taught by . . . history . . . To identify before the fact those characteristics of criminal homicides and their perpetrators which call for the

> death penalty, and to express these characteristics in language which can be fairly understood and applied by the sentencing authority, appear to be tasks which are beyond present human ability.[33]

Can this claim be true at the same time as it is true that capital punishment should be reintroduced where it has been abolished, introduced where it has not yet existed and maintained where it exists? The answer seems to me to be 'Yes'. We can stand in need of a measure or policy that is dangerous unless it is framed properly, and we can lack the resources to frame it properly. In fewer words, we can have a need and have only dangerous or morally illegitimate ways of satisfying it. Many think this is how things stand with the policy of deploying nuclear weapons. Many think that some credible international defence policy is necessary and also that the only one that has been thought of involves the threatened first use of weapons that could not legitimately be used in any circumstances. There is a close parallel between this position and a possible position on capital punishment. It might be thought that while strong threats are needed to deter violent crime or murder, the only credible measure – execution – is wrong to use, for example because of the risk of killing the innocent. To people with this point of view it could seem both necessary and impossible to have some crimes legally punished by death. I do not know whether Kant's theory affords a means of resolving this tension. Perhaps the difference between the possibility and probability of killing the innocent would have to be underlined. I introduce the tension to show within what limits Kant's theory has practical consequences. It recommends the reintroduction of the death sentence, but it does not suggest how the relevant law would have to be drafted to meet Justice Harlan's point.

In what sense, then, is Kant's theory a piece of applied or applicable ethics? It is applicable in a limited sense: it says that, but not how, penal legislation should be changed. It also has a use in helping to transform the content and rigour of the wider debate concerning capital punishment. No one who is exposed to Kant's theory will be inclined to claim, as certain eminent speakers in the 1982 Parliamentary debate were inclined to claim, that retribution is simple revenge. And perhaps exposure to the theory will make fewer people believe that a principle of respect for persons *by itself* rules out capital punishment. Not the least of the changes brought about by applied ethics are changes of mind.

NOTES

1 I follow Bedau, Hugo Adam (1978) 'Retribution and the Theory of Punishment', *Journal of Philosophy*, 75, pp. 601–20 in using three principles from Hart, H. L. A. (1968) *Punishment and Responsibility*, Oxford University Press, as a model of retributivism.

2 Bedau, 'Retribution and the Theory of Punishment', *op. cit.*, p. 611.

3 Kant, *Metaphysics of Morals*, *loc. cit.*, pp. 155–6.

4 See Beck, Lewis White (1960) *A Commentary on Kant's Critique of Practical Reason*, Chicago University Press, p. 154.

5 Robert Nozick tries to supply a general rule in Nozick, R. (1981) *Philosophical Explanations*, Oxford University Press, pp. 363ff.

6 See the General Introduction to *The Metaphysics of Morals*, *loc. cit.*

7 Ladd, *op. cit.*, p. 101.

8 *Ibid.*, p. 29.

9 *Ibid.*, p. 30.

10 There is an interesting sideline to the problem of applying *lex talionis* strictly where judicial error occurs and someone is wrongly executed. What happens in such a case is, if not murder, then as bad as murder, and the people responsible are the judge and jury. So should they pay for their mistake with their lives? If so, then they would be paying very heavily for what is probably an honest mistake, albeit a very serious one. If they escape the death penalty or indeed go unpunished, then there seems to be a violation of the principles of retribution. Under the regime that restricts the death penalty to aggravated murder there would be no inconsistency in not *executing* the judge and jury, but retributivism would still seem to call for some sort of punishment. The reply that the roles of judge and juror insulate the people who fill such roles from responsibility for the acts they commit in these roles is not very plausible. See Nagel, T., 'Ruthlessness in Public

Life', in Hampshire, S. (ed.) (1978) *Public and Private Morality*, Cambridge University Press. I am grateful to John Harris for calling my attention to this point.

11 Hart, *op. cit.*, pp. 234–5.

12 In 'Punishment, the New Retributivism . . .', *op. cit.*, Honderich seems to sympathize with the claim that what he calls 'intrinsic retributivism' makes a good out of two evils.

13 Kant, *Metaphysics of Morals, loc. cit.*, p. 156.

14 See Glover, *op. cit.*, p. 229.

15 Kant, *Metaphysics of Morals*, *loc. cit.*, pp. 145a–6a.

16 *Ibid.*, p. 156.

17 Ladd, *op. cit.*, p. 132a.

18 Kant, *Metaphysics of Morals*, *loc. cit.*, p. 155.

19 Murphy, J. G. (1973) 'Marxism and Retribution', *Philosophy and Public Affairs*, 2; Morris, H. (1968) 'Persons and Punishment', *The Monist*, 52.

20 Duff, to whom I owe the general description of this account, gives Hegel as its source. See Duff, *op. cit.*, p. 258.

21 Ladd, *op. cit.*, p. 132n.

22 Kant, *Metaphysics of Morals*, *loc. cit.*, p. 156.

23 See Duff, *op. cit.*, pp. 211–12.

24 That is, no society satisfying Kant's principle of equality.

25 Murphy, *op. cit.*

26 Bedau, 'Retribution and the Theory of Punishment', *op. cit.*, p. 617.

27 See Honderich, *Punishment: The Supposed Justifications, op. cit.*, pp. 43–4, and 'The New Retributivism', *op. cit.*, p. 140.

28 Stephen, James Fitzjames (1863) *General View of the Criminal Law in England*, Macmillan, p. 99; quoted in Honderich, 'The New Retributivism', *op. cit.*, p. 142.

29 Berns, Walter (1979) *Capital Punishment*, Basic Books.

30 *Ibid.*, p. 154.

31 *Ibid.*, p. 155.

32 *Ibid.*, p. 174.

33 402 U.S. 183 at 204.

Index